A
BITTERSWEET
JOURNEY

A BITTERSWEET JOURNEY

·

America's Fascination with Baseball

Rick Phalen

McGregor
PUBLISHING

Library of Congress Cataloging-in-Publication Data

Phalen, Richard C., 1937–
    A bittersweet journey : America's fascination with baseball / Rick Phalen.
        p. cm.
    ISBN 0-9653846-1-6
        1. Baseball—United States—History—20th century. 2. Sports personnel—United States—Interviews.   I. Title.

GV863.A1 P56 2000
796.357'0973—dc21

                                                            00-025787

"There Used to Be a Ballpark"
Words and music: Joe Raposo © 1973 Jonico Music, Inc.
and Sergeant Music Co. Used by permission.

Cover photo: AP/Wide World Photos.

Interior design and typesetting by Sue Knopf, Graffolio.

Published by McGregor Publishing, Inc., Tampa, Florida.
Printed and bound in the United States of America.

To Griff, a home run in any league,

and Rags, Patches and Kinnon,

great friends

CONTENTS

ACKNOWLEDGMENTS

The inspiration for this book came from a group of individuals all touched by the beauty and drama of baseball. My father, who bought me my first baseball glove, never pushed me to play, but when I was ready he was always available for a game of catch. Lou Rosin, the only coach I had who knew what he was doing and made the game fun. Keith Gerst, who never ceased to make me laugh with the funniest baseball story I have ever heard. Phil Alden Robinson, who awakened slumbering emotions in men from here to east of Suez. My father-in-law, Casey Jones, a major league prospect who was injured playing in the minors and never able to play again, forever scarred by the ordeal, making me realize baseball is a cold-hearted mistress.

Alice Vazquez, who always has sound advice and is a fine friend.

Thanks to everyone who participated in the book for their time and energy in making this a truly great experience.

And a special thanks to those who have taken time to teach youngsters the game of baseball, contributing greatly to their lives and character.

INTRODUCTION

A few years ago, while visiting my old hometown, I went by the ballpark where I had spent many summer afternoons hoodwinking myself into believing I would some day pitch in the major leagues. Approaching, I saw a large building occupying what once was the stage for my small role in the baseball drama. Instead of the green field, the wooden grandstand emitting its mysterious scent in the summer sun and a pitcher's mound that was always too low, now stood a large three story building. Other than a small patch of right field, nothing survived my attempt to embrace the past.

That evening, marooned in middle aged angst, I thought how baseball's siren song lures many to both happiness and despair. As a youngster you become a prisoner of its grace and excitement, and as an adult you maintain the passion, but continue to view the game through the eyes of a 12-year-old. This explains the unacceptable behavior of many fathers at their child's Little League games and their calling Sport's Talk Radio and uttering infantile observations.

With my unfortunate episode fresh in mind, I interviewed others who have been influenced and affected by baseball. I found minor leaguers bitter that they had not made the majors; players such as Bobby Thomson and Al Gionfriddo fortunate to grab that one great opportunity and attain immortality; Leo Durocher, Hal Newhouser and Enos Slaughter with long, distinguished careers sentenced to waiting endless years to be elected to the Hall of Fame.

Seriously wounded, Lou Brissie and Bert Shepard returned from World War II and performed at the major league level; Jimmy

Piersall had a nervous breakdown playing ball, but came back to become a truly outstanding player.

The young boy who waited for his father to return home from working for the railroad to have a catch, only to witness his death; how the movie *A League of Their Own* brought back memories and tears to Dottie Collins, an ex-All American Girls Professional Baseball League player; Vin Scully describing the tremendous price you pay being in the game because on the road you spend time "killing" one of the most precious things you have—time—and as you get older how it weighs heavier and heavier. How drugs ended Dock Ellis's career; Dave Filken singlehandedly losing the Pony League Championship for his team; Roger Kahn's reason for writing the classic *The Boys of Summer;* and Phil Alden Robinson, the writer and director of *Field of Dreams,* discussing his tremendous film.

Pam Postema, convinced baseball is determined to keep women from umpiring; Dave Pallone's ordeal as a gay umpire; Richard Topp's obsession with researching baseball deaths; David Clyde, expected by many to be a star, instead finished his career disillusioned and with a losing record. Jackie Warner, like thousands of others, had a few weeks of stardom, then never saw the big leagues again; Gar Miller explains why he owns four million baseball cards; Jonathan Winters as "Bad Boy Lenderhoffer"; and middle-aged Keith Gerst describes how as a child he followed a cowboy movie hero from the ballpark after a World Series game and the star uttered a vulgarity that bewildered him; and much more.

I wrote *A Bittersweet Journey* to illustrate that the game is more than reading box scores, attending three games a year, and the fond reminiscence of playing catch with one's dad. When baseball leaves the happiness of the playground it becomes organized, and organized baseball is a business, and like all businesses it is based on profit and loss, and that is when it becomes deadly serious. The game, on close acquaintance, has equal parts melancholy, bitterness, disappointment and fun.

Baseball is more than a game, it is the American experience. It is competitive, tough, loud, informal, racially diverse, theatrical, spectacular, heroic, financially rewarding, and an excuse for a bunch of people to get together and raise hell. A foreigner once said, "To understand America you must first understand baseball."

A Bittersweet Journey will leave the reader with a better understanding of baseball and America by explaining what we do during the summer in America, why we do it, and the consequences. It is, as Vin Scully told me, "the best game ever invented."

You see,

you spend a good piece of your life

gripping a baseball

and in the end

it turns out

that it was the other way around

all the time.

JIM BOUTON

INSIDE THE LINES

JIMMY **PIERSALL**

At the start of the 1952 season, during his rookie year with the Boston Red Sox, Manager Lou Boudreau started Jimmy at shortstop. He had never played the position and did poorly. After appearing in only 56 games, of which 22 were in the outfield, he had a nervous breakdown. He was placed in a sanitarium, but recovered in time to appear in 151 games in 1953—all in the outfield—and hit .272. Quite a comeback.

I had a lot of problems (with the fans). In Detroit, we were playing a night game. I come to the plate and we got the bases loaded and the count goes to 3-0. It's the 11th inning. I looked down for the sign and Del Baker gives me a take. Look down again, I'm taking again and the pitch was kind of low. I looked back at Flaherty and now the count goes to 3-2. I take the next pitch and I couldn't hit it with a 9 iron. He called it strike three and I eat his butt out. But he don't throw me out. As I'm going to the outfield they're throwing all kinds of debris. They peppered me. They stop the game and it takes about 20 minutes to clean the field.

So here comes McKinley (Bill McKinley—umpire) out and he says, "You're an instigator, Piersall." And I said, "I don't know what that means, but they shot the wrong McKinley." He threw me out.

Why were the fans in Boston so hard on Ted Williams?

They were tough on him, but you know why? They sort of sensed that when they got on him, he played better. He hit better. Ted used to say to me when I got mad about something, "I'll

3

take care of it kid. Don't worry." He used to talk through his teeth when he got mad. I said, "Ted, why are you getting so mad all the time." And he said, "You know why? Because I've got to be good every day. You don't have to be."

We used to pump him up by turning the heat up too high. He didn't like the heat up. We went and turned the heat on before he'd come into the park. April or May was cool. He'd get mad as hell.

I hated the movie *Fear Strikes Out* because it was not the Jimmy Piersall Story. My book, *Fear Strikes Out* by Al Hersberger, was done about me. When they bought the property, they rewrote the whole thing for Hollywood. The only thing that was right was where I lived as a kid. The rest of it was all rewritten. I didn't climb any screens. My father wasn't that awful bad on me. I was a little bit highstrung, but they made me a "whacko." Nothing to do with my life.

Perkins was a great actor, but he was no baseball player. He was skinny; they had to put shoulder pads on him.

You know one of the funny parts of that? Perkins was left-handed. They got Tommy Holmes to teach him how to throw right-handed. He (Holmes) was a left-handed thrower.

The other teams weren't on my ass about the movie. They were on me when I first started, and then Mr. Yawkey made them stop. I said, "Mr. Yawkey, they don't bother me."

They were calling me gooney bird and blowing sirens at me and stuff. I found out that when they do that I'm a good player. Manager Mayo Smith of Detroit forbid his players to get on me, 'cause he said, "Don't wake him up." The more they hollered at me, the better I played.

Dick Williams used to sit on the bench in Baltimore and go . . . "Coo-coo, coo-coo." I said, "Yeah, but I'm playing."

I loved Frank Lary. He was always on me.

We used to draw big crowds, the Red Sox and Detroit, on weekends especially. I hit a home run into the lower deck on a slider off him and the next time up he threw me a curve ball and my ass flew out and I let my bat go and it went by him on the mound. He went over and picked it up. As he handed it to me he dropped it and I bent over and he kicked me in the ass.

The umpires had a different attitude. It was show business to them. One time somebody ran across the field and Ed Runge said, "There goes your crazy brother." I didn't like that. I got pissed. He got suspended for a week.

I never played shortstop in my life. I hated it. I remember sliding into second base and Phil Rizzuto said to me, "If you could play a year in the minor leagues you'd be a great shortstop." And I said, "I don't want to be no fuckin' shortstop." He said, "Well, what are you doing here?" I says, "I've gotta feed my family." I got so goddamned keyed up that I wound up in the sanitarium. They gave me shock treatment and it really did a job. I have no recollection of that place at all.

I'm not blaming Boudreau. It was coming on from pressure anyways, because my mother and father were old, I had kids and I wanted to be a major league player. In my day, there was a lot of guys. You know, we (Red Sox) had something like 15 minor league clubs.

Mr. Yawkey sent me to Florida with my family and I worked out with George Susce, one of our coaches, in 1953. I was so afraid I said, "George, I don't know if I can hit the ball again. I don't know if I can even catch it I'm so scared." Well, I got to working out and I had the biggest break any kid could get. The third game of spring training we're playing the Dodgers. And listen to this lineup: Catching—Campanella. First base—Hodges. Second base—Robinson. Shortstop—Pee Wee Reese. Third base— Cox. Left field—Shuba. Center field—Snider. Right field—Furillo. Pitcher—Erskine.

I go five for five. Five for five and make a couple of catches. They've got me playing right field. And that was the turning point in my whole career.

Susce kept telling me when we were working out, "Jim, you're going to be the right fielder. You're a great player." 'Cause my instincts off the bat, nobody had any better instincts than I had.

I was a great studier of opposing hitters. A great study of what they did previous. I had great ability to read my own pitcher, what kind of stuff he had. Watching the catcher set up, where he was setting up. I had the great ability to move the other outfielders with me. I'd drive Williams crazy.

Williams was great because in those days we didn't have padding on the wall. I used to study the opposing walls on the road and at home and I knew just how far they were from certain areas. I had great sixth sense. I always had that good, quick look. But I needed a guy like Ted 'cause I had pretty good speed and he used to holler, "Lotta room. Be careful." Oh, he was great at that. That's a gift.

When I started playing with Ted he was getting up in age, but he had great hands and he moved good. He knew how to play the hitters, too. In his book he called me the best outfielder that played next to him, and you know Dom (DiMaggio) was a great fielder. And to have him say that, that's better than being in the Hall of Fame.

You played for Casey Stengel when you were with the Mets.

Casey used to fall asleep in the 5th inning. Duke Snider just joined us from the Dodgers. We were sitting at the end of the bench and we're getting beat 9-0. Koufax has got about 10 strikeouts and finally he says, "Go get him." So I run down, and the grounds crew is dragging the infield and I go, "Hey!" Casey jumps up giving signs to the grounds crew.

Stengel didn't know where he was . . . which was most of the time. He never knew your name. I'll tell you the rest of this story. Now, we go to the ninth inning. He's looking for a pinch hitter. He never knew your name. It was, "Hey you, kid. Hey you, boy." He never knew who the hell you were. So he's looking for a pinch hitter and who in the hell wants to go hit against Koufax. So I said, "Hey, Duke, he wants you." So Duke goes up and he's got 399 home runs. And on the second pitch he hit it out of the Polo Grounds. Over the left field fence. He's a left-hand hitter.

So now, the next morning I buy the papers and there's only

a little clipping in there that he'd hit his 400th home run. I come into the ball park and I was a smart ass and I said, "Hey, Duke, I thought you were a big man in New York, in Brooklyn. You're going to be in the Hall of Fame. All-Star. World Series star. Look at this. You hit your 400th home run and you get this little bit. I got 99. When I hit my 100th home run I'm going coast-to-coast."

Now, we're playing on Sunday afternoon and we got a full house. The Mets used to draw. Those fans used to come out to see how bad we could get on weekends. They always had those big signs—they had poster contests. I tell the photographers to keep an eye on me today. Now, I haven't hit a home run in two years and I'm going to hit one today. But I didn't tell the writers. We're playing the Phillies. Dallas Green is pitching and we're in the seventh inning and the score is 2-0 and there's two on and the first pitch comes in and "pfff"—I hit a little fly ball down the right field line. You know it's only 257 and 259 down the lines in the Polo Grounds. The next pitch I hit a little fly ball down the right field line just foul again. The count finally goes to 3-2 and I hit a high fly ball just inside the Chesterfield sign 247 feet away, and I run backwards.

Now, the next morning I know I'm going to get some ink, and I wake up at 5:30, and in those days in New York they had eight papers. I buy them, and not only did they have a sequence of me running around backwards, they had it on the front page of every paper including the *New York Times*. So I bring copies into the ballpark and I said, "See, Duke. I told you I was going coast-to-coast. And if you don't think so, I'm going to be on the Jack Parr Show with Zsa Zsa Gabor dropping quarters."

Stengel released me. What a break. The next year I get the Comeback Player of the Year with the Angels and I sent him a small trophy and told him to stick it up his ass. I said, "The only good thing about Stengel is you ought to put a chain on him and let him run around the top of the dugout."

• • •

A lot of guys in baseball I can't feel too sorry for. When they got through, they went home. Most of the guys I played against and with, a lot of them were alcoholics. Baseball athletes today, despite all the other baloney are far better, far superior physically than we were. They don't know how to play like we did 'cause they don't serve their apprenticeship like we had to.

We may have been better. We knew how to play, we had better instincts because we played more when we were kids. We used to play every day as kids. Then we had to play four to five years in the minor leagues to get to the big leagues. These guys today are learning their trade, many of them, in the big leagues. But the fans have accepted that because half of the fans in the stands today are women, which is great, 'cause they're really helping to save baseball, but they really don't know when a player's doing much wrong. You get the old fans watching a ball game and boy, they really tell you.

Baseball was my life when I was a kid. Basically, all of my life I've been in baseball. I ran a football team, though, for three years in Roanoke, Virginia, for Lombardi. That was an experience. Like a AAA minor league club. And I've run hotels. I've had food brokerage businesses. I've done everything to survive.

Any kid today that can play baseball is far better off. They have places to play, but you don't see them out there playing any more. You see them doing a lot of other things. They've got cars and bicycles and things to go to. They've got television to watch and they've got more toys and they've got amusement centers. I think the ruination of our youngsters today is all those places where they can play those machines.

I used to play between buildings. I used to play with bottle caps. I learned to hit the ball with bottle caps. That's why I was such a good breaking ball hitter in my day. Hit the curve ball off a tennis ball.

In those days you always knew every player. I can't name the players on every team. You can't either. But in our day, you only had eight teams in each league. Boy, you could remember the players.

BOB **CAIN**

On August 19, 1951, the St. Louis Browns were playing the Detroit Tigers at Sportsman's Park, St. Louis. In the bottom of the first the Browns' lead-off hitter, Frank Saucier, was lifted for a pinch-hitter by the name of Eddie Gaedel. Gaedel was three feet seven inches and 65 pounds—a midget.

Bob Cain, the Tiger pitcher that afternoon, remembers it well. He walked him on four pitches, but believes Gaedel would have swung if the ball had been in the strike zone. Trouble is, he didn't have a strike zone.

Eddie Gaedel had his moment in the sun, but his sun set on June 18, 1961, when he was beaten to death in Chicago, his assailant or assailants never found.

The Detroit Tigers played the St. Louis Browns in a doubleheader, August 19, 1951. The Tigers won the first game 5-2. Before the start of the second game, the Browns held a promotion on the field.

Bill Veeck put on the promotion along with the Falstaff Brewery. He had mentioned he had something special planned for that day, but nobody knew about it. Between games Bill Veeck had a big doins' around the infield; Satchel Paige was playing the drums and Max Patkin was on third base with his antics and they put on quite a show. Pretty soon there was a big 4-wheeler coming out on the field. It was one of those big paper cakes. It got up by home plate, stopped, and out jumped this midget, Eddie Gaedel. All three feet, seven inches of him.

Eddie Gaedel goes over and sits in the dugout and we proceed to warm up to start the game. They got us out in the first half of the inning. When I went out on the mound to warm up, Zack Taylor motioned for the umpire, Ed Hurley, and they announced that Eddie Gaedel, wearing number ⅛ was going to pinch-hit for Frank Saucier who had started in right field. As they announced Eddie Gaedel to bat for Frank Saucier, Hurley wanted to know what was going on. As Hurley started to walk over to the Browns' dugout, Zack Taylor, the manager, came walking out and pulled the contract out of his hip pocket and showed it to Hurley. Everything was in order; even showed the time that he had sent it to the league headquarters to verify that they had room on the roster for another player. Hurley took a look at the contract and come back and yelled "play ball."

In the meantime, Bob Swift (Tiger catcher) came out to the mound and was talking to me. We were trying to figure out a way to pitch to the midget. I didn't know whether to throw underhand, try to get one over, or just what to do. We were joking around about it a little bit. Bob goes back to home plate and he lays on the ground and puts his hand on his head to give me a target. Ed Hurley didn't like that very much and he made Swift get up in his regular stance. Even though Swift got down as low as he could, I still threw four pitches too high for him.

I was afraid to throw too hard, afraid one might get away from me and hit him and thinkin' that he could not get out of the way. With Swift down on his knees the way he was, the pitches would have been high enough for a strike on an ordinary batter.

We were both laughing about the situation at first. I was trying my darnedest to get one pitch across the plate. Bill Veeck said he would have shot the little son of a gun if he would have swung at a pitch. Eddie, when he went up to bat, stood like Joe DiMaggio with his feet spread far apart and he was crouched over. Actually, I don't think I had a strike zone.

I think if one would have been down another foot or so, he might have swung at it. But I know one thing, if he would have swung and hit it, it would have knocked the bat out of his hands. He had a bat that was about 10 inches long. One of those miniature bats.

I ended up walking him and they put Jim Delsing, the regular outfielder, in to pinch run for Eddie Gaedel. If I remember right, Cliff Mapes was the next batter and he got a base hit. Then I walked Kenny Wood, and I had the bases loaded with nobody out. But I turned around and got out of the inning without any runs and we won the game, 6-2. I pitched eight and two-thirds innings and Dizzy Trout relieved me.

Will Harridge was the president of the American League at that time and he was furious. The next day he banned midgets.

He banned not only Eddie Gaedel, but all midgets in the future. Veeck said, "Well, heck, there was no restriction. Look at Phil Rizzuto, who's just a little over five feet." At that time there was no restrictions in the rule book in regards to the height or the size of the player. Bill mentioned later that his next feat was to get a giant—(the) tallest man he could find—to put in.

The thing that gets me is people only remember me as pitching to the midget. I had my first major league start against the New York Yankees and I beat them 15-0 in their home park. That's when I was with the White Sox, and then I turned around and beat them four times that year.

Bob Feller pitched his third no-hitter against me. I was with Detroit in 1951 and I lost that game 2-1. Then a year later, in 1952, when I was with St. Louis, Bob Feller and I tied up again and we each pitched a one-hitter and I beat him 1-0. So I halfway got even with him. Kind of gets lost in the shuffle.

Eddie Gaedel was murdered in Chicago in 1961. He was drinking quite a bit and fell in with the wrong crowd. He went out one night and came home all beat up and his nose was turned over on the side and everything. His mother asked him what happened and he says, "Well, if I'd known you were going to ask me all kinds of questions, I wouldn't have come home." She called the doctor. Their family doctor was out of town and another doctor came and took a look at him and says, "Oh, he's just drunk, so leave him alone. Maybe he'll sleep it off." Well, early in the morning, around 4:00 A.M. or so, Eddie's mother went in and took a look at him and foam was coming out of his mouth and he had died.

My wife and I were the only two from baseball who went to his funeral.

BOBBY **THOMSON**

On August 11, 1951, Robin Roberts of the Philadelphia Phillies beat the New York Giants 4-0, dropping them 13½ games behind the Brooklyn Dodgers. From this point to the end of the National League season the Giants won 39 out of 47 games. They tied Brooklyn for the pennant and went to a three game play-off, splitting the first two games. Game three saw the Giants down 4-1 going into the bottom of the ninth.

"Branca throws . . . there's a long drive! It's going to be, I believe! The Giants win the pennant! The Giants win the pennant! The Giants win the pennant! The Giants win the pennant! Bobby Thomson hits it into the lower deck of the left field stands! The Giants win the pennant! And they're going crazy! They're going crazy! Oh-ho . . . I don't believe it! I don't believe it! I do not believe it!"—Russ Hodges, October 3, 1951.

On August 11, 1951 the New York Giants were 13½ games out of first place.

We hadn't given up, certainly. Not with Leo Durocher at the helm. We showed up, put on our suits every day and went out to play ball. We weren't too happy being that far behind, because at the start of the season we had higher hopes for ourselves. We kept showing up and, of course, if you played for Durocher you better be ready to play. There was no quitting.

Aside from our tremendous streak, Brooklyn lost their share of ball games. If they played better than .500, I don't think it was much over that. So, we needed them to lose their share.

We tied Brooklyn that last weekend, on a Friday night. We were a half game behind the Dodgers and they had three games with

Philadelphia—Friday, Saturday and Sunday. We were up in Boston to play Saturday and Sunday. The Dodgers lost to Philadelphia on Friday night. I went to bed that night and I think my roommate, Whitey Lockman, and I must have felt the pressure because we didn't have the best night's sleep. I remember waking up Saturday morning and we didn't even look at each other. We came down in the elevator, got in the lobby and the place was full of people. Finally, I remember our eyes met across the breakfast table and we both burst out laughing. We really didn't feel a thing until we became tied. You know, when you're behind, you're under a certain amount of pressure, but the real pressure to me is on the front runners.

It was down to two games. They won Saturday; so did we. Then we won our game on Sunday and we were in the clubhouse and the Dodgers were losing. The Dodgers were losing by quite a few runs it seemed to me—around the sixth inning or so. When we got on the train headed for New York late that afternoon, we thought we were the winners. I'll never forget—we found out when we got off the train the Dodgers had won. Jackie Robinson had played the game of his life, making a great play to save the game . . . to keep it tied in the last of the ninth. Then he won it with a home run in extra innings. I'll tell you, the bottom just dropped out for us. At least it did for me, 'cause I didn't look forward to playing those guys.

In the first game we were losing 1-0 and I hit a home run with a man on base, something like the fourth inning, and then Monty Irvin hit a home run later, so we won 3-1. That was against Branca.

We moved over to the Polo Grounds and Clem Labine—we just couldn't do anything with him and I think the closest we came was when I got up to bat with the bases loaded and he struck me out. We lost 10-0.

In the third and final game it is the bottom of the ninth and you are behind 4-1. Newcombe gave up a single to Dark and then a single to Don Mueller. Lockman doubled, scoring Dark, the score now 4-2. Hodges was not playing off the bag as he should have

with a three-run lead when Mueller hit the ball. It was a ground
single to right instead of a double play ball and you would have
not gotten to bat.

Dark's base hit was just a ground ball right through the middle. You know, just out of the reach of everybody. And Mueller's
was the same thing. A ground ball to right which Hodges dove
for and just missed by less than a foot. He was playing on the bag.

We would have been dead. That's just the way I felt going into
the dugout the end of the ninth inning because Newcombe had
looked so good in the eighth inning. And I thought, "Heck, I'm
the fifth hitter. I'm dead. I won't even have a chance."

When Lockman doubled to left and scored a run, Mueller went
into third and hurt his ankle severely and it stopped the game.
Mueller's lying on the ground and he's hurt. He's in pain. I'm
down there with a bat in my hand and a great concern about him.
It took my mind right off the game. Just for a few minutes. It
wasn't until they carried Don off the field on a stretcher that I
got back into the ball game.

I remember when I walked to home plate. I never approached
home plate from third before. Walking back to home plate I
started talking to myself: "Get up there and give yourself a chance
to hit. Do a good job. Wait and watch. Wait and watch." And all
the time I'm calling myself an S.O.B. Now I'd never done that
before in my life. First of all, I don't know if the word is "numb,"
where you're going through the motions. Looking back at it, it
seemed to me you just followed your instincts. You're a ballplayer
and you know what you have to do. And that's what I did. I just
kept telling myself, "Wait and watch. Don't get over-anxious. Do
a good job, you S.O.B. Give yourself a chance to hit."

As I'm walking back to home plate, all of a sudden I realize
Newcombe's not the pitcher. Branca's on the mound and it didn't
faze me one way or another. I just got in the box waiting and
watching him.

Jeez, if he doesn't throw the first pitch right through the middle. I was waiting and watching too damn much. The guys later
told me—the guys on the bench—they wanted to kill me for tak-

ing a pitch right down the middle. Now, Ralph . . . his idea, I guess, was to come inside with a fast ball and then make me hit a breaking ball away. But he got it inside and it was a bad ball, but it wasn't bad enough for me not to get around on it. I was quick with my hands. I was hitting the ball pretty well. I got a glimpse of it and I jumped on it. It was a fast ball inside.

I thought I had a home run. I made good contact and I saw it take off and I thought *home run*. I've never hit a ball like that in my life before because it started up in the upper deck, but then had tremendous overspin. I obviously got a little bit on top of it. It started to sink, and when I saw it start to sink I thought, "It's not a home run. It's a base hit." But then it didn't take long for it to disappear, because I hit it pretty well. I was halfway down to first base, then that was it.

I was kind of hyperventilating running around the bases. I wasn't running my normal home run trot. I felt like I was prancing around the bases. I've never experienced excitement like that before in my life.

Running around the bases, all I remember is as I got to third, Durocher kind of reached out for me and I just casually pushed past him. I guess Stanky by that time was coming out and grabbing him.

I remember hitting home plate. All the guys were there waiting for me. I took one last leap—I didn't run across it, just one last jump on it. We're all heading to the locker room and the next thing I knew Lockman's got me up on his shoulders and we're heading out to center field. And, of course, the people started to crowd around. That went on for a bit and finally, Whitey thought we'd better forget this stuff and get in the locker room.

Branca and I get together once in a while. We've become friends and we've gotten to know each other.

After baseball, I had to get a job and go to work and bring up my family and just become an ordinary citizen. Got involved, you know. Always like to think of myself as having been brought up being responsible. I've gotten involved in my community just like any normal human being does. I consider myself lucky to still be remembered for having my day in the sun.

JIM **BOUTON**

n 1970 he wrote *Ball Four,* and it caused an uproar. It was the first "tell all" baseball book, and he stepped on a lot of toes and egos. The book revealed that many ballplayers were not in the mold of Jack Armstrong, but rather prone to take a drink, pop a pill, chase women and engage in other bacchanalian pursuits. It also revealed that a fair number of the players of that era were not, upon retiring, going to become brain surgeons. This was the period before free agency, and management treated the players much like chattel and were penurious to a fault.

Why did you write Ball Four?

I went away to play baseball at the age of 19 and came back after my first season of professional ball in the minor leagues and told my family and friends what a crazy and fun experience it was and they all said the same thing . . . you ought to keep notes and write a book some day.

The owners didn't like *Ball Four.* I realize now it had nothing to do with locker room secrets. It had to do with the fact that *Ball Four* was the first book to tell people how difficult it was to make a living in baseball. This was before free agency, and the owners had the players locked up. Had us tied to whatever team we were signed, and we had to stay with that team for the rest of our career unless they traded us. We had no say in the trades. So we had to sign whatever contract they gave us. They took advantage of it and they would pay $10,000 or $15,000 to guys who played in the major leagues three to four years who were good ballplayers.

The year I was 21 and 7, my salary was $10,500. I talked about
this in *Ball Four* and showed how the owners took advantage of
the players. The owners and the commissioner were afraid that
a judge would read this book, or a jury, or an arbitrator, or a con-
gressman or something, and baseball might lose their anti-trust
exemption. The irony is that's exactly what happened in 1975 at
the famous Andy Messersmith arbitration hearing in New York. I
was the only former player called to testify against the owners.
I read passages from *Ball Four* which was accepted as legal evidence because it was based on contemporaneous notes.

So the owners were afraid of the economic impact that *Ball
Four* might have on their game. The players had a different reaction. They believed the baseball commissioner when he said this
was bad for baseball. But if they had read the book, they would
have realized that it told the players' view of the game.

We had a very restrictive contract and we were not getting our
fair value in the marketplace. That was pretty clear. The owners
were stealing our money and they said they needed to do that
in order to maintain competitive balance. That was a lie, because
once there was competitive balance in 1975, when ballplayers
became free agents, there was actually more competitive balance.
The Yankees were winning the pennant just about every year
under the old system, and under the new system of free agency
they had more teams winning pennants. So they were wrong
about the reason they were tying us to teams.

Some sportswriters were jealous of the access that I had to
meetings and other private goings-on that they didn't have access
to. A lot of sportswriters were selling the "milk and cookies" image
and they felt that's what they ought to do, and here was somebody coming along telling everybody, in effect, that that was all
nonsense. So it sort of put a lie to their work. These guys . . . it
was their life's work. Sort of painting pastel colors every year, so
they were angry at me and jealous.

More kids (during my day) were signed directly out of high
school and right off the farm. They would sign at 18 and play
minor league baseball so they really weren't exposed to that

much. Even though they traveled around the country, in most cases they were not inquisitive people. They didn't go out and look around the town. They didn't travel. They didn't explore. They didn't sightsee; they basically stayed in their room or went down to the pool hall or whatever. They hung together and were isolated in a sense. Some of the guys weren't that bright.

There were other guys who had been to college and had been away, and some had been in the service and they were much further ahead of the kids who had just signed out of high school. You had more of a mixture of guys when I played ball. Today, most of the players have been to college for at least one or two years, and some for three and four years. The players today are much smarter, as a general rule, than we were.

Part of what made *Ball Four* a successful book is that the time was ripe for it. It was a time in which the nation was questioning itself. In the early sixties we sort of had our eyes closed. By the end of the sixties we realized that Vietnam was a mistake and that our leaders had misled us and a lot of people were lying about our role in the world. We were starting to questions things—question the old order—and that's when *Ball Four* came out. It was a period of great awareness . . . emerging self-awareness.

Ballplayers didn't read it because it was 400 pages and there was nothing to color in. Most guys didn't read books when I played ball. Somebody would read a book on the bus and he would get a nickname as "Professor" or something like that. You were a genius if you got caught reading a book. Most guys didn't even like to read the newspapers. Joe Schultz [his manager in Seattle], when I asked him if he wanted to read the first part of the newspaper, said, "No, I don't read that section."

There's something about standing on the mound with a ball in your hand and the challenge of seeing if you can throw it sixty feet, six inches into this little square space and keep this other guy from hitting it. There's something challenging and fun about that. I'm sure it's the same for the batter. A baseball game is really a series of challenges. It's 120 challenges by each pitcher, 'cause that's how many pitches you throw . . . so you're putting yourself on the line 120 different moments. When you add them up for both teams, that's 240 different moments of potential drama in a game. You hardly have that in any other sport.

I didn't write *Ball Four* as a crusade. I wasn't thinking of doing something that might catch flack. I wanted to write all this stuff down so I could share it with people and have the memories myself. If I hadn't written that stuff down, I would have never been able to recall it. I can just crack open the book any time I want and read whatever's on that page and it brings back these wonderful memories.

AL **GIONFRIDDO**

The 1947 World Series between the New York Yankees and Brooklyn Dodgers is considered one of the most exciting ever played. There were three stars in that Series: Bill Bevens of the Yankees who pitched a no-hitter for eight and two-thirds innings; Cookie Lavagetto who broke up Bevens' no-hitter with a double to win the game; and Al Gionfriddo who in game six made a tremendous catch against Joe DiMaggio to kill a Yankee rally. Gionfriddo's spectacular feat would forever more be known as "the catch."

Al Gionfriddo never played major league baseball again. He stayed in the minors until 1956, finishing in Class A ball. Ironically, neither Bevens nor Lavagetto ever played in the majors again.

I was traded from Pittsburgh to the Brooklyn Dodgers. I thought I was being traded from a great team, 'cause I thought the Pirates had a chance of winning everything. But the Dodgers won the National League that year. We played the Yankees in the 1947 World Series. What I remember most about the '47 World Series is that Bill Bevens had a no-hitter going in the fourth game and the Yankees were beating us 2-1. Carl Furillo walked and I went in to run for Furillo, 'cause I was a pretty good runner. I used to run the 100 in 10 flat. Pete Rieser came in to pinch hit for Eddie Stanky. The count was two balls and a strike on Rieser and I got the steal sign. I stole second base. So they walked Pete Rieser intentionally. Then Eddie Miksis ran for Rieser. I don't believe that Bucky Harris, the manager of the Yankees, knew that Pete Rieser had a cracked bone in his ankle and couldn't run, or else I think he would have pitched to him.

21

Then Cookie Lavagetto come up to pinch-hit, and the second pitch he hits off the right field wall, and I score from second and Miksis scores from first and we beat the Yankees 3-2 on Bevens' one-hitter.

In the sixth game you made that great catch of DiMaggio's drive to left.

When I looked in at the dugout, Burt Shotton, our manager, was moving me more toward the line, figuring that DiMaggio's going to be pullin' the ball. The way they were pitching him, it didn't make sense to me. But anyhow, he was making me play toward the line a little more. The Yankees had two men on and we were leading 8-5. When Joe hit the ball, he hit it exactly toward the 415-foot mark by the left field bullpen and, like I say, I was playing pretty close to the line, so I just turned and ran with my back toward home plate, looked once over my shoulder and I knew I wasn't near it, so I had to keep running. When I got to the bullpen gate I looked up over my left shoulder with my back toward home plate and jumped and caught the ball over my left shoulder. As I caught the ball, I turned in the air and come down and hit the bullpen gate, which was about four feet high. We ended up winning that game. There was two men on when DiMaggio hit the ball. If it's a home run, it's a tie game. They went on to get one more run. They would have beaten us 9-8. But as it was, we ended up beating them 8-6.

I was happy. Everybody was happy . . . saved a home run. Come into the dugout and everybody beat on my back. Beat me so bad I didn't know if I was going to get to the plate. Anyhow, I was the first hitter and Allie Reynolds was the pitcher. He could throw that ball . . . looked like an aspirin coming up there.

You know, everybody remembers the catch, but very few people remember the stolen base that helped to break up Bevens' no-hitter, because there's not too many pictures out on it. But there's pictures of the catch. They had the cameras there.

Branch Rickey was a money-hungry owner. He calls me into the office to sign me the next year before spring training. They bring out all the stats that you did for them during the year. My stats wasn't great that year, 'cause I didn't play that much. I pinched-hit, I run and I played defense most of all, because we had some outfielders who could hit and run and throw, but they couldn't catch too good. So late innings when we were ahead, I was playing defense in the outfield.

So, anyhow, he called me into the office to sign my contract and he wasn't there. So I talked to his son, who they called "Twig." I didn't sign the contract. My mother was pretty sick in the hospital and was going to get her leg amputated and they call me at the hospital and tell me either you sign or we're going to spring training without you. So, I took a train back into New York and signed the contract.

Well, all during spring training, everything went well. I had a *good* spring training. We get to Brooklyn, now we're going to play Montreal in an exhibition game. The game was rained out and my wife and I went to the movies. We came back home. We're listening to the news and I hear that I was sent down to Montreal. So I go over to the office and Rickey wasn't there and his son wasn't there. Nobody wanted to talk to me. And I said, "Well, I guess I gotta report to Montreal." And that was it.

Then, I finally got a hold of him on the phone and he says, "Well, if you go to Montreal, and you have a good year, we'll bring you right back up." So I did. I went down and hit .330 at Montreal, had a good year, I didn't get called back up. He said, "Well, you've gotta have another good year to prove it." That's the way they were in baseball. So I had another good year and I still didn't get called up.

I played a couple of more years in Montreal and they were good years. Never went back to the big leagues. Then they asked me to go down to Fort Worth to help Bobby Bragan who was one of the catchers with us in 1947. I went down and helped Bobby Bragan as a player-coach and then after that I managed a few years in minor league ball and then I moved out to California.

I am very bitter. I think I was so mistreated. I missed getting my pension in baseball by sixty days. Nobody would bring me back up. The Dodgers never brought me back up. And it really made me mad and I've been hurt, but you gotta live with it. It's long gone. Can't look back. But I wrote to 'em, I called 'em; they promised me so many things, it wasn't even funny. Buzzy Bavasi, who was the general manager at Montreal, promised me if I would go to Montreal with his team that he would bring me back to the big leagues if he went to the big leagues. Well, as you know, Buzzy Bavasi went to the big leagues as general manager for years. He brought Walter Alston up. I never got back up there. Seems all he kept doing was promising. When they moved out here to the coast I went down and talked to Buzzy, and he says, "Al, we'll make you our bullpen coach. We're going to see that you get your pension." No way. He went to San Diego, same thing. I kept talking to the Dodgers, Frisco Thompson, all of them. And for some reason, they never ever wanted to bring me back. Sometimes I'm sorry I ever made the catch, because if I would have never made the catch, I think I would have stayed in the big leagues.

"You'll be a great drawing card in Montreal for us. You go there and have that good year and we'll bring you back." Well, I had a great year in Montreal and they never brought me back. He said, "Well, you have another good year and I'll guarantee we'll bring you back." Well, I had a good year. I hit .330 and he still didn't bring me back.

I always called baseball the Chicago Stockyards. The owners could do anything they wanted with you back when I played. We went out on strike in 1946 in Pittsburgh to get a union started. We wanted a base salary. We wanted some kind of insurance to protect us for our families. We were playing the Giants a double header and we refused to go out on the field. We had an attorney and Branch Rickey and Horace Stoneham—we were playing the Giants and Horace Stoneham was the owner of the Giants—wanted to know why we wouldn't go out. He said, "We're going to fire all of you ballplayers." We said, "Well, go ahead. You can't fire the whole team." He said, "What do you want?" We said, "We want you to meet with our attorney. We want a base salary for a rookie and an insurance policy, some kind of protection." So, they agreed to it. And they met with our attorney and they worked it out and the next year we had a base salary of $5,000.

When I first went up all I made was $5,000.

CLANCY **WOODS**

From age seven he was convinced that he would play in the majors. He signed with the White Sox while in college and played in their minor league system until being unceremoniously released. He is one of thousands.

I was signed by Bruce Andrews, a scout in Los Angeles for the Chicago White Sox. He had coached in organized baseball for a number of years. That was my first experience with negotiating.

Got a bonus. I got a total of $10,000 and realized that I left probably $15,000 or $20,000 on the table. That's why I say it was my first lesson in negotiating, because I gave them the old "If you'll do this, I'll sign today" routine. I learned that that was not the best thing to do.

Went from there to rookie ball in Sarasota, Florida. I remember thinking, *Hey, I'm pretty hot shit. This is a big deal. I'm a professional athlete now.* That lasted until I got my first check and realized that I was a professional athlete taking home $356 a month.

That was after my junior year in college at UCSB . . . 1977. Went down there and played with a number of really talented players: Rusty Kuntz, who later played with the White Sox. Rusty was a center fielder. Just a tremendous ballplayer. A. J. Hill, Rich Barnes were on our team. We won the league. We were 51-13.

The coaching was much to my surprise very laissez faire. I had expected a lot of coaching, a lot of instruction. But it just never happened.

From Sarasota—rude awakening number two—I went to spring training. Had a good spring. Fully expected to go to the Midwest League, which was Appleton. Class A.

Actually, was sent to an independent team in the California League. And the independent team had four or five players from the White Sox, four or five players from the Cubs, some Indians players, and it was the guys apparently the White Sox thought were on the fringe. It was strange to me 'cause here I was, the first player taken in the eighth round by the White Sox the year before. I go my first year—don't get any instruction. I go to spring training—throw well and apparently I'm not on the A-list. So I'm going to the California League and I figure I've had adversity before so I'm just going to show what I can do.

It was the Bakersfield Outlaws and it used to be a Dodger farm team. Well, the Dodgers blew out of there years before and so they (Bakersfield) did anything they could to get a minor league franchise. The best they could come up with was an independent club. And I mean, we didn't have uniforms. The manager was guy named George Culver who pitched for the Phillies and the Reds in his major league career. Threw a no-hitter against Cincinnati, by the way. But we got there and they didn't have enough players to fill out the roster. So they signed local guys. One of the local guys had polio as a kid and had one leg about three inches shorter than the other. Couldn't run. He's our catcher.

Just really a bizarre collection of characters. A bunch of eight-balls from different organizations. Guys that either had attitude problems, or were discipline problems, or guys that nobody ever paid any money to, or real low-round draft choices. It was probably the funnest experience I had in baseball. We're outcasts of some sort and we had something to prove. I mean, the White Sox said, "Hey, we don't want to release you, but we don't think you're any good, so go play on this independent team."

One of the guys made it to the big leagues, a guy named Gary Krug. He went up with the Cubs briefly. We won 43 games and lost 97. I had a great time because I won 13 of the 43 games. I was 6-0 against the two division winners. Four and zero against the Dodgers and 2-0 against the Visalia Twins. We had a ball. We had so many fun things happen. It was a very close-knit group. It was *Bull Durham* before *Bull Durham*.

Came back to Santa Barbara for the off-season. Went to spring training in Sarasota and thought based on the year that I had I was definitely going to AA, possibly AAA. I was very disappointed when I was assigned to Appleton (Class A), which is where I thought I should have been the year before. I was in Appleton for about two weeks and they had me in the bullpen. I was throwing the ball very, very well and the minor league pitching instructor made a stop in. I pitched several times while he was there. I wasn't even there a month and was sent to Knoxville, our AA affiliate in the Southern League. Went up there for the balance of the year.

Knoxville, I had mixed results. At times I was great, at times my inexperience as a pitcher showed. The level of play was up a considerable notch over A-ball. The lack of a third pitch—I threw a hard fast ball, sinker-slider—I didn't have a change-up. That made a big difference. I was 6-6 there with a handful of saves. But I played on a team that had some outstanding players. Richard Dotson, Britt Burns, LaMarr Hoyt. Our pitching staff was those three, myself and Larry Monroe, who was a Chicago kid who was up with the White Sox when he was 19 and was back down. Fascinating experience. It was really an eye-opener to see the level of play increase as much as it did.

What happened the next year?

Went to spring training. Pitched two and one-third [innings] and was released. This was 1980. I was pissed because here I am, 22 years old. I thought, this is a raw deal. This guy with this great arm. As good an arm as anybody in the organization and they told me I'd get all this instruction and they would close the gap, give me some experience and, of course, it never happened. I really felt like the White Sox didn't uphold their end of the bargain.

Of course, when you're that age you really don't have any experience dealing with business people and how it works. You don't really know how to deal with that. Your anger and your disappointment. I was bitter . . . I was a pissed-off kid.

The last thing I expected was to be released. I was very disappointed that I only got to throw two and one-third innings. The year before when I was with the White Sox A-club, before I got promoted to AA, Bruce Dal Canton was our pitching coach. To give you an idea of how volatile this is, I was throwing so well that at one point early in the season the White Sox went north with eight or nine pitchers. They had an injury or whatever and they needed somebody to pitch in the big leagues, like the next day. Well, I had just thrown the night before. Bruce Dal Canton was recommending that I go to the big leagues and pitch this one-game start and I couldn't go because I'd just thrown. I'd thrown like 130 pitches and they took somebody else. You wonder . . . I could have gone up there and got shelled, who knows. On the other hand, I could have gone up there and thrown a four-hitter.

So it was like it didn't even matter. They'd made a decision a long time ago. They didn't even look at me. They weren't paying attention at all. I didn't understand that. I really didn't understand all of that and when you're a young guy, and from the age of seven you know that you're going to be a major league baseball player, you're not thinking about any of this stuff rationally. It's all emotional. I wasn't prepared to understand it as it really is.

Do I want to roll the clock back and take one more shot and show the bastards that they made a mistake? Yeah. But I also think that that's part of what drives you to be great in whatever else you do.

MONTE **IRVIN**

H e played for the Newark Eagles in the Negro National League from 1937 to 1948, with time in the service from 1943 to 1945. Monte believes the Negro Leagues were equivalent to AAA ball and believes each team had two or three players who could have played in the majors. They played under tough conditions, with none of the amenities of the major leagues. Rosters were small and anything went—from the "spitter" to playing under portable lights.

Monte came up to the New York Giants in 1949. By that time the Negro Leagues were on their last legs, the majors now taking their best talent.

Monte Irvin was an outstanding player. He was called to the majors when he was 30 and played until he was 37, time enough to be elected to the Hall of Fame.

You began your career with the Newark Eagles in the Negro National League.

I lived about twenty minutes from Newark. The owner, Abe Manley, scouted me and another fellow and wanted us to play for him. I was still in school; I was a little hesitant. He said, "Why don't you play under an assumed name?" So I did. I started (in) '37 with them on the road, after school was over. Then I graduated from high school in '38. So I played '37 and '38 with them on the road.

When they played at home, I'd work out and then go sit in the stands. Communications were not as good at that time, so if you played in Pittsburgh, Rochester—nobody would know. A lot of guys were doing the same thing, trying to earn a few dollars, because bucks came very hard during that era.

They would do anything to entertain, to draw fans. They used to have portable lights. They started with portable lights back in '36, in there some place. It was a combination of entertainment and pure baseball. I would say each club would have two or three guys that were real major league material. You had six teams in the Negro American and the Negro National League. Then maybe two or three independent clubs. Clubs like New Orleans, Houston and Atlanta and two or three others. They were independent, but they were still pretty good. It was a good league. It was about AAA.

Each club around that time had sixteen to seventeen guys. That's all. The saying was, "You're in there forever, 'til the game is over. The game is yours." If a guy really got knocked around, they would put an infielder in who had some pitching experience, or somebody else who could get the ball over the plate and just get the game over. In fact, I used to go in and pitch. I came up as a pitcher.

Say we've got a doubleheader. We've got two or three pitchers we could not use. The guy would go all the way the first game. The second game, if the pitcher got in trouble, we'd use the guy that was rested the longest, and the starting pitcher for the first game might go in the outfield and play. All of us could play just about every position. We were very versatile. I used to catch and my buddy would pitch, and then in the second game, vice versa.

When a minor league team was away—the Newark Bears, the farm club of the Yankees—that was our home field. They arranged the schedule like that. Same thing with the majors. Polo Grounds, Yankee Stadium and Ebbets Field. When they were away, we'd play over there. So we're at the complete mercy of organized baseball. The reason they didn't mind was they got good rentals and they controlled the park and the concessions. We were just tenants.

We drew pretty well. In a major league ballpark, sometimes we would have 25-, 30-, 40,000, say Satchel Paige against Raymond Brown. Satchel Paige against Willie Foster or Satchel against Leon

Day. They would emphasize pitching duels. Buck Leonard, Josh Gibson and three or four other guys were really publicized. Cool Papa Bell, Sam Bankhead and right down the line. Guys like Rap Dixon, Biz Mackey, Louis Santop, Oscar Charleston, John Henry Lloyd. These guys were still playing—playing and managing. We had about ten or fifteen guys that could have been Hall of Famers if given a chance.

I was a good player before I went into the Army. I came back with war nerves. I signed with the Dodgers along with Roy Campanella and Jackie Robinson. I told them I wasn't up to par and wanted to play myself back into shape. I wanted to get the feeling that I used to have. I came back September 1, 1945—right away I went to Puerto Rico to hone my talents. Started to come back and by 1948 in Cuba, I was scouted by Alex Pompez. He was scouting for the Giants. He signed me and Hank Thompson. The next year we reported to Jersey City. We went to spring training in Florida with the Jersey City Giants, a farm club of the New York Giants and [I] was called up first of July.

It was a matter of getting your confidence. The ball wasn't that much better. All my life I'd been told I wasn't as good or couldn't play in the majors. So once you got your confidence you found out that it was easier. You could expect the ball a certain place. A pitcher got in trouble, he's going to throw his best pitch. Playing conditions were much better. The food. The training facilities. You'd get a rubdown. I never did get a rubdown 'til I got into the majors.

We used to rub each other. If a pitcher got sore, another pitcher would rub his arm and right down the line. We took care of ourselves.

I called the Dodgers and told them I was ready to report. The lady who owned our club, Effa Manley, said, "You just took Newcombe and you didn't give me anything for him. I'm not going to let you take Monte and not give me something for him."

She's talking to Rickey. She said, "I'll fight you in court." She hired a lawyer. So rather than have a big lawsuit and bad publicity, because Rickey never paid any money for any black ballplayers that he signed, including Jackie—Jackie, Campanella, Newcombe or myself—he never paid a nickel. But she wanted $5,000. So he said to her, "I'm not going to do that." She said, "Rather than get into any kind of hassle, I'll release him." So they released me. Alex Pompez signed me and everything started to really improve.

Hitting, running, fielding and throwing—I was second to none before I went into the Army. They said the best arm they'd ever seen. Great fielder, lot of power. Big and strong and could run like a deer. Had two years of college and I got along with people.

Temperamentally I'd be all right 'cause I played in the integrated system in Orange High School and throughout the state. I was used to playing in an integrated situation. It didn't bother me one way or the other.

I didn't have too many problems with the ballplayers. Maybe one or two on the club, but you don't pay them any mind. They were just happy to be in the majors themselves. But the fans were kind of rough. We heard all the names and treated to all kinds of crazy ways. So, we were used to that. We used to barnstorm down South, so we'd seen everything and practically heard everything. So that didn't bother us. Emotionally we would play harder and take it out on the ball, and they would say these things when the game started and by the time the game was over they were rooting for us. We played real good and made them like us.

Philadelphia was rough. St. Louis. Cincinnati. Wrigley Field just a little . . . in the outfield. The bleacher bums would give you a pretty rough time. They were the roughest.

You couldn't stay in a hotel—even in Chicago and Philadelphia and St. Louis, too. Pittsburgh, not too bad, 'cause there's a lot of black people in Pittsburgh. Boston wasn't too bad. The rest of the cities were pretty good. But the ones I mentioned were the rough ones.

In '54 the hotels were integrated. It came about because at the Chase Hotel in St. Louis, Jackie Robinson walked into the dining room. He was hungry and wanted to get something to eat and he didn't feel like eating up in the room. See, we could come to the lobby, get a paper, get our key and go right to the room and then order room service. So, he said, "What the hell, I'm tired of eating in the room. I'm a good ballplayer, one of the leading players in the league. Why not eat in the dining room." So he went in and sat down. The waiter came over and said, "What do you want?" He said, "I want to get served just like everybody else." The waiter called the manager over and the manager said, "Well, what's the problem?" He said, "I want to be served just like everybody else." So the manager said, "Go ahead and serve him." The word got around the league and that broke that down. Then we started to stay with the club in Chicago and the other cities and nobody died, no problem. It was just a matter of somebody doing it.

You once said, "Baseball has done more to move America in the right direction than all the professional patriots with all their cheap words."

It's true. When Jackie succeeded it opened up opportunities in all the other sports. It helped more black secretaries, teachers to be hired . . . mailmen. It made it better socially, economically and every other way. I knew that would happen.

DOCK **ELLIS**

He was a fine pitcher who won 138 games in the bigs, including a no-hitter. He always spoke his mind, which irritated management. No one owned Dock Ellis, but "greenies" had a mortgage on his body and soul. There was a long period when he was always high at the ball park, whether he was pitching or not. Drugs ultimately ended his baseball career.

But Dock did something about his addiction. He went through substance abuse counseling and therapy and has turned his life around.

My father always taught me I was my own man. Nobody could tell me anything, as far as what to do. A lot of people are threatened by the fact that if they don't heel to the demands of the company, then they don't have a job. My thing is there's a whole lot of jobs out there. So no person or company can tell me what to do. That's the way I went through baseball, because I knew as long as I threw a baseball and threw it well, then somebody would want me no matter what I said.

The Pirates at one time tried to put a muzzle on me, but that was futile. They started going to players and telling the players to stay away from me. That didn't do any good because it didn't shut me up, and as far as any influence I had on anyone, what I was speaking was the truth.

We had a very close-knit team. People accepted me for being Dock. It wasn't until we started trading guys in from other organizations where someone might question what I was saying or what I was doing, but the ones that had come up in the organization with me would soon straighten them out. They would say, "He's only saying what we all want to say." I remember one time when they suspended me for not going to the bullpen, one individual said, "Well, Dock, they own us." I said, "No, they own *you*. They don't own *me*."

When I refused to go to the bullpen toward the end of '75, Danny Murtaugh was coming back [as manager] and Joe Brown had to get rid of me. Danny didn't want me back. I guess he felt he would lose face with the team if I were to come back after I refused to go to the bullpen. When Joe Brown got rid of me, it wasn't something that he wanted to do, it was something he had to do. He explained that to me and to the press. He also explained it to the New York Yankees and won money because he made them a bet that I would win over 15 games for them (he was 17-8 in 1976).

George Steinbrenner and Billy Martin—I got along well with the two of them. You know, George Steinbrenner is a person who wants to win at all costs. I always tell people, "If I'm trimming your grass and you pay me $20,000 a month, and you come home and your grass is tall and your trees aren't trimmed, what are you going to do?" He pays an outfielder $2,000,000 and he throws to the wrong base, he's supposed to raise hell. You're paying hitters two and three million dollars and the man on third base is dying there with less than two outs. You're supposed to drive in runs, he's paying you to do that. I don't give a damn if somebody's out there throwing softballs, you're supposed to drive that run in, not strike out.

Billy Martin, Dock Ellis and George Steinbrenner talked plenty shit. Talked shit to each other. We never had any run-ins. Other than when I was getting ready to leave. They said that I stated George Steinbrenner was traveling with the team so much that one day he might go down on his airplane, something to that effect. I never made the statement. But sportswriters say they heard me say it. George Steinbrenner knows who made the statement and the person who made the statement I just saw and I told him, "Man, they had that thing in the paper again." He said, "Ha, ha, ha, ha."

At the beginning of the 1977 season you were traded to Oakland.

The end of my career. Something was going on with my hand. I didn't know what it was. A nerve problem or something in my finger because in '76, in the playoffs, my finger was having spasms and it was a nerve in the arm. I was also involved more into drugs at that particular time. I had gotten into drugs really heavy then. That was the downfall of my career, from '77 to '79.

I grew up playing around with drugs. But when I got into base-ball the drugs were more readily available for me because of the fact [of] where I was going and who I was associating with at that particular time. It's just that I had better connections, let's put it that way.

The drug of choice for baseball players at that time was Dexamil, to supposedly enhance your play. But individuals were abusing Dexamil—the "greenie." But there was a lot of marijuana and a substantial amount of cocaine around the league.

I really got into it around '76, real heavy. I was in pretty good shape. God gave all us good athletes good bodies. So I just destroyed my body, but it was strong enough to withstand all the drugs then.

I lost all interest in baseball, I'd rather be high than play base-ball. When I came to a game and I wasn't pitching, I had to get high just to be there. I couldn't sit there and watch a baseball game. I don't ever remember not being high. One time I tried to pitch and was not high; I had to run back to the clubhouse and get some Dexamil.

[Dexamil] made me feel that I could thread a needle with a base-ball. It made me think that I could throw hard. Some times I was thinking I was throwing hard and I wasn't throwing hard. Sometimes I was throwing hard and thought I wasn't throwing hard.

Management knew about everyone that was involved with sub-stance abuse. If you're successful, why mess with it. That's all everyone ever cared about, was winning. That's the American way —at all costs.

I don't wish I could do it over again. If I had to go back and live my life I would want to live it the way that I lived it, because if I didn't, I wouldn't be the person I am today. I don't regret nothing that I've ever done. If I go back and I don't get into drugs, I'm going to be screwed up somewhere down the line because I wouldn't take a look at myself. But having gone through substance abuse counseling and therapy, rehabilitation, I had to take a look at myself. And I love me today. You know, I would have never seen that if I hadn't been in drugs.

DOTTIE **COLLINS**

She pitched for the Minneapolis Millerettes and the Ft. Wayne Daisies of the All American Girls Professional Baseball League from 1944 to 1950. The league was the idea of Phil Wrigley—one of the few he had—to provide entertainment during the war.

The girls played good baseball and the league drew approximately one million fans annually. The league folded in 1954 due to lack of fresh talent and competition for the entertainment dollar. But for one shining moment they made an impact.

I originally played *baseball* in 1944, but I played a lot of softball prior to that in Southern California. In fact, I started playing softball in 1936. Went over to hardball in 1945.

When the All American Girls Professional Baseball League started in 1943, the ball size was 12 inches. The base paths were 65 [feet] and the pitching distance was 40 [feet] and it was underhand pitching. Then each year, the ball got smaller, the base paths got longer, and the pitching distance got longer. We went underhand through 1945, and then went side arm in 1946. We went to complete overhand in 1948. By the time the league ended in 1954, we were playing with a 9-inch ball . . . that's a regulation men's baseball . . . 85-foot base paths, a pitching distance of 60 feet.

I was one of the fortunate ones. I converted very easily. A lot of the girls were not able to convert. One of our greatest fast pitch pitchers, Connie Wiesniewski, was not able to convert. She just couldn't throw the overhand baseball. She was a great athlete, so she went to the outfield and became one of the great outfielders of the league, along with [being] a great hitter.

39

P. K. Wrigley had an idea that the war was going to last a long time and he was going to pull the girls into the major league parks. There were games held at Wrigley Field and at Yankee Stadium. Exhibit-type games. In fact, they won't admit it, but we played the first night game at Wrigley Field. There were temporary lights put up and it was a game between the All American Girls Professional Baseball League and the WACS and the WAVES.

I entered the league in 1944. I played for the Minneapolis Millerettes. They didn't last. We became the Minneapolis Orphans by mid-season and lived in a bus, you might say. The following year that franchise was sold to Fort Wayne, Indiana. I played through 1950.

Rockford Peaches, South Bend Blue Sox, Kenosha Comets, Racine Belles, Milwaukee Chicks, Minneapolis Millerettes, Fort Wayne Daisies, Grand Rapids Chicks, Peoria Red Wings, Muskegon Lassies, Chicago Colleens, Springfield Sallies, Kalamazoo Lassies, Battle Creek Belles and the Muskegon Belles were in the league.

After the movie [A League of Their Own] came out, I received many phone calls from reporters and television people from all over the United States. I did nothing but answer the phone for about five days. Just about everyone told me the same thing: "We thought this was a farce until we saw the ending of the movie and saw you gals at the age of 65 and 70 out there playing an old timers' game. If you can play that well at that age, you must have been terrific when you were kids."

That was an actual game that was being played at the end of the movie when they were running the credits. Those were actual All American Girls and the average age of those women on that field was 65 years.

We drew over a million a year. That's on an average of eight to ten teams in a league. Except for the first year. There were only four teams in the league the first year. That's what the movie was based on.

The movie was quite accurate. The only thing that wasn't accurate was the manager and we call that the "Hollywood Flair." They had to have that in there. But we never had a manager like that. I think they were trying to pattern it after Jimmy Foxx, who everybody knows was an alcoholic. But Jimmy did not act like that, and he was a gentleman at all times with the girls.

But, the rest of the movie . . . the bus trips . . . seeing the bus going down the road, that really brought a lot of tears to a lot of eyes. That was very, very accurate. The little boy on the bus—that actually happened, although he wasn't quite that mean. The young man coming to Cooperstown to honor his mother who had passed away, that happened. We didn't all live in one dormitory. We lived with families in our member cities. People took us in, generally two girls to a home and a chaperon. They were our mothers away from home and they were not depicted very well in the movie. We felt kind of bad about that. But other than that, it was very, very true, except they couldn't play as good baseball as we did.

They didn't develop a farm system. When the war started there were fast pitch softball teams all over the United States and Canada, especially on the East and the West Coast. When the war came those leagues disbanded because of blackouts. They couldn't play at night. We used to draw 5,000 to 7,000 a night out in Southern California. It was a great deal. So with those fast pitch leagues disbanding they weren't creating any new players. The war ended and TV came into the picture and people had money in their pocket and it just didn't go.

They had no new girls. Most of the girls that were playing in the end were either new girls that hadn't had that much training or girls that had been in a league too damn long and were getting too old.

When we played there was gas rationing and all that stuff. People were looking for something to do, especially families. We drew families.

We have formed a nonprofit organization and I am on the board of directors. I'm the treasurer and I answer the phone a lot. Everything basically comes through here. All the mail comes through here and all the phone calls come through here.

We have an annual meeting once a year. We try to have a national reunion every two years. We meet here in Fort Wayne, normally, every year . . . a group of us . . . maybe a hundred of us in September in conjunction with a woman's sports "Run, Jane, Run" deal, and we play a reunion ball game.

The legs are the first things to go. We can all throw and we can still hit. I can't—I never could. But the majority of the girls that were good hitters can still swing the bat. They can field. But they can't run. The legs just won't go.

It's been very rewarding for all of us. It's brought a lot into our lives. It's been amazing because when we first started out and got together in 1982, we had no idea this was going to happen. It has kept going and going and going and I don't know where the end is.

We have a lifetime roster . . . 559 [that played]. It is on computer and we have a listing of every girl at Cooperstown, which was a big thrill for everybody because our names are at Cooperstown.

GENE **HERMANSKI**

The Brooklyn Dodgers started a rookie at first base in 1947. He was a tremendously gifted player and would be named Rookie of the Year. Two years later he was voted the Most Valuable Player in the National League. He could do it all.

But for the privilege of playing in the majors, he had to subject himself to virulent abuse. Not only from opposing teams, but from fans and a few of his teammates. During his first year it was rumored the St. Louis Cardinals were not going to take the field against him.

His name was Jackie Robinson, and Gene Hermanski, a former teammate, recalls that time.

I'll tell you, '46 I had a horrible year. I became very selfish. I'll tell you why, because if I don't play well in '47, I'm out of there. Ended up hitting .165 or something [.200].

My job was on the line. Whether Robinson's red, green, black, yellow—I didn't give a damn because I wanted to remain in the big leagues.

I think that eighty to ninety percent of the guys accepted him. There was Dixie Walker, Hugh Casey, Kirby Higby, maybe others [that didn't]. These were the three outstanding ones. In fact, Kirby Higby and Dixie Walker were traded in '47, Casey in '49. But myself and maybe eighty percent plus of the guys accepted him like anybody else.

I remember one time in Ebbets Field, before the game we were working out in the infield. Ben Chapman [Philadelphia's manager] was in the dugout and he saw Pee Wee Reese and Robinson working out at short and second. He yelled over to Pee Wee,

"How do you like playing ball with a nigger bastard like that Robinson?" Pee Wee heard him, but he made believe he didn't. So he kept easing towards Robinson. He finally put his arm around him and embraced him and said, "What did you say, Ben?" That kind of shut him up.

Enos Slaughter was notorious about getting on his back. Several others, but those two stand out in my mind. Slaughter and Ben Chapman.

He became a little aggressive after two to three years in the big leagues, which I don't blame him. How in the hell would you like to hear this every day, "Black jack, shoeshine boy?"

In Cincinnati we had our team meeting and Burt Shotton said, "We got a serious thing here. Robinson got several threatening letters. There's like sixty to seventy FBI men and cops, detectives, in the stands because they threatened his life." Shotton says, "I want you guys to be aware of this. Under the circumstances, if anything happens, at least you're aware of it." He says, "I'm stuck. I don't know what the hell to do. Does anyone have any suggestions?" Everybody paused and looked around. I raised my hand, he says, "What do you want, Hermanski? What have you got to say?" I says, "Well, it's very easy, Burt." He says, "What? What's very easy." I said, "All we've gotta do is change our numbers. Everybody wear 42. They wouldn't know who to shoot."

[In] '47 he's Rookie of the Year. Within three years he makes MVP. Now what in the hell . . . who could beat that? I could see if he failed miserably. But he did it.

Robinson couldn't stay in the hotels with us. Someone would contact a lawyer or doctor of Negro extraction and explain the whole thing to them and they'd be more than willing to say "Yes [stay in private homes]." And of course, they would compensate whoever accepted him for the time he was there.

It was very competitive and we were very hungry. Hungry ballplayers. We weren't making much money, but who knows what big money was in those days. When you read in the paper somebody's making $50,000 and all of sudden you read about Joe "D" and Stan Musial and Willie Mays and Ted Williams making

$100,000, you say, "Jesus Christ, that's something to strive for." That was a lot of money in those days.

I always wanted to do better, of course. You always say to yourself, "Why can't I hit the ball as frequently as Stan Musial or some of the other good hitters." But I finally figured out those guys are at bat ten times. They hit the ball well eight times. Not [all] base hits, [but] they hit it well. But guys in my category would maybe fall off to five or six times out of ten. Hit the ball well, get some good wood on it.

The hand-eye coordination and the instinct of catching the ball, the instinct of getting a good jump on a ball, you can't teach that. You can't teach a guy to run fast. You can't teach him how to throw hard.

I was well aware that Dixie Walker disliked Robinson and didn't want to play with a black. But I can remember one game—I think toward the end of the game, eighth or ninth inning—Walker said to someone else, which I heard very clearly, "He may be black, but he's a good fuckin' ballplayer."

We were at spring training. I could run pretty good. I always felt down deep in my heart in a 40 to 50 yard dash I could beat him. So I says, "Hey, Jack, I want to race you." He says, "What do you want to race me for?" I says, "Well, I feel as though I can beat you." He says, "Maybe you can, maybe you can't. But it'll never happen, because I've got nothing to gain. If I beat you, I'm supposed to beat you. But if you beat me, it'll be in all the papers." So he smiled and walked away. I got along real well with him.

LOU **BRISSIE**

Lou was severely wounded in Italy during World War II. He was hit by shell fragments from a German 170mm gun. His left leg, ankle and right foot were broken, and he had shell fragments in his hands and thighs. He was in such poor condition, and his Army doctor performed such exceptional surgery on him, that the doctor was given a medical commendation by the Surgeon General, and in September 1947 Lou was playing for the Philadelphia A's. His combined record for the '48 and '49 seasons was 30-21.

At a time in our history when victimization is almost a national obsession, Lou Brissie's career is an inspiration. He fought a war, was severely wounded, overcame his handicap and competed at the major league level. He didn't complain about being victimized, he just went out and did his job.

America needs all the Lou Brissies it can find.

I enlisted in the service in December '42. I was injured on December 7, 1944 in the Apennine Mountains in Northern Italy. I was hit by artillery fragments from a 170mm gun. I was hit in the legs, in the hands, both thighs. My left leg was broken severely. My left ankle and right foot were broken.

It's always been kind of hazy. This happened about 11:30 A.M. and I vaguely remember being at a battalion or regimental clearing station for medical cases at dark. Then of course they send you to a field hospital, but the more severe injuries they evacuate quickly. I was flown back to the 300th General Hospital in Naples.

The day I got there I remember Major Brubaker came in and looked at my chart and told me he would be my doctor and I told him, "I don't know what you're gonna have to do, but don't take my leg off because I want to be a ballplayer, and I have been, and I want to be again." He didn't say anything. He was looking at the charts and going through everything and he glanced at me and said, "Well, we'll see." But he never promised anything. He didn't say, "Don't worry." He just said, "We'll see."

He told me he did over 3,000 orthopedic procedures while he was over there. I was very fortunate to have gotten him. He did some exceptional things and the Surgeon General gave him a medical commendation for the work he did on me. He said that in World War II there were thousands of cases similar to mine and normally they were amputations. I was fortunate not to have been.

They flew me to Casablanca and then to the Azores and then to New York. We had to wait for the weather. Back in those days it took five or six days before they got the weather they wanted for us to start back. Then from Mitchell Field, where we landed, they flew me to Finney General Hospital in Thomasville, Georgia. I was in Finney, and then went to Northington General in Alabama. I was discharged in the summer of '46.

Amazingly, you tried out with the A's in September.

I didn't try out very long. I was only there a few days and my leg got infected and I had to go to Valley Forge Hospital right outside of Philadelphia.

Mr. Mack told me, "When you feel that you're ready, let me know and I'll see that you get a chance to play ball. Find out whether you can play or not." I let him know and he had me report to West Palm Beach with the ball club in February '47 and I stayed with them through spring training. On the way north they had two options. They could have sent me to Buffalo or Savannah, in the Sally League. Mr. Mack said, "I own Savannah and I can guarantee that you'll pitch regular and find out if you can hold up or not." So that's the one I picked. He let me choose.

I had a good year in Savannah. I believe I finished the regular season 23-5.

Well, I did pretty good in '48 [14-10 with the A's]. I had not relieved very often in Savannah. Tom Oliver and Jimmy Adair always told me, "When the fourth day rolls around, you're the pitcher." I might relieve in between, but not a lot. But in Philadelphia I did a lot of both. I came through in good shape.

From time to time I had a little difficulty, but I think that's true of anybody in sports. I just had to change everything I'd ever done. That was the hard part. I didn't look like the same pitcher. I didn't throw the same. I didn't stride the same as I did before I was hurt. I used my left leg, the one that was severely injured . . . I didn't really push off. I just kind of pivoted on it and tried to take a long slow motion. You develop limitations that you become accustomed to. But for the most part, I did all right. From time to time it would give me trouble, but not on a regular basis.

In 1949 you were 16-11. Then in 1950 you fell to 7-19. What happened?

I think that was maybe one of the better years I had. I lost several games 1-0. At the break for the All-Star Game, I was something like 2-12. I'd had a little difficulty over the winter and had osteomyelitis.

It is an extremely serious bacterial infection of the bone marrow that comes with those type injuries. It was troubling me and I got a poor start. Things just didn't seem to work that year. I lost some tough games and I did a lot of relieving. I pitched something like 240 [246] innings. I did not pitch after the first week of August.

The last few years I've thought more about how fortunate I was to have had that disability and still make it up there because I think it was one of the better times baseball has had in the last 100 years.

By the time I got there Mr. Mack [Connie Mack, manager] had been around a long time. He was very low-key. But he would come up with an attitude toward people about somethin' [and] you just couldn't change his mind. I heard him make some very, very wise statements in the heat of a ball game when you get a couple of guys that maybe goof up on something and are having a few words at each other because they're upset. One time we had a couple of guys upset and his only comment was, "Gentlemen, in the heat of battle, words that are spoken do not apply or should not apply"—something like that. He was good to play for, although he didn't do it in a hands-on fashion. Jimmy Dykes was kinda his go-between in a lot of things.

He always deferred to Mr. Mack. But Mr. Mack, as he got older, would have difficulty keeping up with some of the things. And Jimmy would say, "Mr. Mack, if this next pitch is a ball, it's going to be 3-1. What do you want him to do?" Sometimes I would call it prompting, but Jimmy had too much respect for Mr. Mack to try to lead him. Right at the end it got very difficult for him.

He called that '48 ball club his greatest club for effort. He said he'd had great ball clubs, but he'd never had a greater ball club for spirit and effort than the '48 club. Although we finished fourth, we were in that thing right up to the end [84-70, 12½ games out].

You were traded to Cleveland during the 1951 season and stayed with them through 1953.

I had a big disagreement with Mr. Greenberg [Hank Greenberg, GM-Cleveland]. They got waivers on me during the World Series in '53 and held my contract until February first, which was the last day for contracts, and sold me to Indianapolis. People I knew in the Cleveland front office let me know that Baltimore and the Giants were trying to buy my contract.

I always felt I had an obligation to a lot of guys in the service who were not as fortunate as I. I got a lot of letters from fellows who said, "Hang in there." I felt an obligation to them and to a lot of friends that I had left overseas to give it my best. I said, "Hank, I am not going to fade away into the minor leagues when I know I can pitch major league ball. I know there are clubs that want me." He said, "How do you know?" I said, "Doesn't matter.

I just know." He said, "Well, you'll play there or you won't play."
I said, "Well, then I won't play."

I felt I could pitch and evidently somebody else thought that.
I decided I would walk away and that's what I did. I didn't look
back. I always loved it. I missed it to a degree. But I didn't regret
it because I felt it was the right thing to do.

BERT **SHEPARD**

He flew a P-38 during World War II, and while on a strafing run over Germany was shot down. The Germans pulled him from the wreckage but had to amputate his right leg. As a result he was returned to the United States in February 1945.

Incredibly, he joined the Washington Senators the next month and in August 1945 pitched his only major league game . . . with a prosthesis!

His stats:

Innings	5.1
Hits	3
BB	1
SO	2
ERA	1.69

Few guys that play organized baseball ever make it to the majors. Bert made it with one leg.

On May 21, 1944 you flew a combat mission over Germany that changed your life.

I had started a baseball team over there and our opening day was May 21, 1944. I'd flown about four out of the last five days and I wasn't scheduled to fly, but I saw it was a pretty tough mission—all-out strafing—so I said, "Well, let me fly on the mission and I will still be back in time for the ball game." We went in deep, almost to Berlin, and let down on the deck and come out shooting up trains and stuff. There was an airfield ahead that had some airplanes on it so I got down real low, about twenty feet off the ground, and when I was about a mile from the airfield I must have passed over an anti-aircraft gun. They shot my foot off and then

I got hit in the chin and as I was coming to, I pulled back on the wheel and couldn't make it. I crashed going at pretty high speed. I remember nothing until I come to in the hospital in Ludgwigslust, Germany several days later. They had amputated the leg and there was about a two-inch piece of skull above my right eye that was missing. I was awful lucky to come out of that alive.

I stayed in the hospital about four weeks. Then I went to another hospital in Wismar on the Baltic Sea and that was the finest hospital I've ever been in. They had a great staff there and great equipment to work with. Then from there I go down to Hoemark, near Frankfurt. That's for interrogation, and then I go to two more camps. These are sort of convalescent homes. We had a bunch of amputees, broken backs and burn cases and stuff. Then we assembled, got ready for the prisoner exchange which took place at the Swiss border. The German prisoners of war who were amputees and injured badly came over from Canada and the United States. At the Swiss border we got on their train and they got on ours. Incidentally, their welcoming home present was a picture of Hitler and an apple. Ours was a little better than that when we got to the States.

I have to say I received more competent medical care as a prisoner of war then a lot of the care I've received here in the States. Their doctors were extremely professional and very skillful.

We got on the *Gripsholm* in Marseilles, France around January 23, 1945. We had to stay in dock a couple of weeks and then got to New York, I believe February 21.

While I was in prison camp, a Canadian prisoner by the name of Don Airey made me a crude artificial leg and I was able to practice running and pivoting and walking on it in prison camp. I got to New York February 21 and was sent up to Walter Reed Hospital. March 10 I got a new leg, and March 14 I joined the Senators.

Under Secretary of War Patterson invited four prisoners to come down for an interview so he could make a press release and tell the public how we'd been treated and what to expect with the prisoners still there. After the interview he asked me what I'd like to do and I said, "Well, if I can't fly combat I would like to play baseball." He said, "Oh, you can't play baseball can you?" I said, "Yes. With this leg made in prison camp I've got an idea what I can do. With a better leg I'm sure I can run pretty good." So he called Clark Griffith, the owner of the Senators, and said, "I've got a guy here that's just back from prison camp and has a leg off and says he can still play baseball. Could you give him a try-out?" So naturally Mr. Griffith is very obligated with the Under Secretary of War calling and he said, "Well, whenever he's ready to come out, tell him to come."

They were training at the University of Maryland, which was very close to Walter Reed. They gave me a uniform and I went out on the field and started pitching batting practice and one of the reporters said, "Who's that out there? That's a new one." Somebody said, "Well, that's the guy just back from prison camp that has a leg off." Well, you couldn't tell it by watching me unless you looked very closely. He got on the phone and called the other news media and said, "We've got a pretty good story here," and within a couple of hours there was newsreel people there, a lot of photographers and reporters and it made a pretty big splash.

You got into one game in 1945. You pitched five and one-third innings, gave up one run, three hits, one base-on balls and had two strike-outs.

I came in with the bases loaded and George Metkovich was the batter and I struck him out. So I got by pretty good. Playing the Red Sox at Griffith Stadium.

I felt very confident. Of course in any kind of a competitive sport you never know what the outcome will be but you do your best and I was fortunate enough to get the boys out. The reason I got in there is they'd scored about twelve runs and the score was like 12 to 3.

We were fighting for the pennant and we had four knuckle ball pitchers and they were all pitching pretty good. The last day of the season we were waiting in the clubhouse to see if the Browns would beat the Tigers, because if the Browns beat the Tigers, we're tied and we had to go to Detroit for a playoff. So it was real tight and all the other games were very close and we were winning, so I never had a chance to get in.

I pitched in several exhibition games and in spring training. I pitched a total of twenty-three innings with the Senators . . . something like that, including the regular major league game and exhibition games. I allowed about three to four runs in the twenty-some innings. We played New London Navy Base on a day off, an exhibition game, and Yogi Berra was with the team. I started, pitched five innings, allowed one run and three hits. The regular pitchers came in and they scored twelve runs off of 'em.

I went to spring training [the next year]. I pitched three innings twice, allowed no runs, no walks and one hit. I thought, "Well, I'm doing pretty good here." But we had a lot of players back from the service and that's the only time I got in.

I stayed on as a coach, hoping to get on the regular roster later on. It looked like I wouldn't make the regular roster. I asked them to send me down to Chattanooga, which is AAA. I went down and won two and lost two. The first game I shut the team out for seven innings and squeezed the only run of the game home in the seventh inning and a relief pitcher came in and finished. So I won the first game 1-0.

At the end of the '46 season I barnstormed with the American League All-Stars and I pitched and played first base against Feller's All-Stars. I got two for four off of Feller. Went one for two off of Sain and I was playing first base.

I went to the hospital then to get a re-amputation, to have the stump shortened to about seven inches below the knee, because the Germans cut it off with the idea of having plenty to work with.

In Walter Reed they fouled the amputation up and I had to have four more over a period of two and a half years, so that just about wiped out my baseball career. The only job available in 1949 was managing Class B. I was a player-manager and played first base and pitched and I think I won five and lost five. I hit four home runs, though, and stole five bases.

I went down to manage St. Augustine in '51, but my arm wasn't any good from being on crutches that two years; I got a lot of muscle that I didn't need.

An Englishman who was in the service in World War II was hunting in Hungary with a German doctor who didn't speak English, but the Englishman spoke German. They're talking about what they did in World War II and the German said, "Well, during the war I picked up a Bert Shepard out of an airplane crash and took him to the hospital and I wonder what ever happened to him." The Englishman said, "By God, I'll try to find out." So he sent a fax to a friend he knew was a pilot in World War II. He didn't know me, but he knew a P-38 pilot in Texas. *He* didn't know me, so the P-38 pilot in Texas sent it to a P-38 outfit in California and they had me on the roster. They sent that information to the Englishman and he called me up to see if I was the one he was looking for.

I wrote a letter to the German doctor, asked him a lot of questions and he sent me a nice letter back which I had to have interpreted. He said that they were being heavily strafed and bombed that day and he went to a flack tower. One of the Germans was killed and the other was wounded bad and he had a hard time getting him down. Then he was directed to go to my wreck and I was unconscious in the cockpit. The Germans were going to take care of me—the farmers—'cause a lot of them had been strafed, and he had to pull out a gun and chase them away. The little hospital in Ludgwigslust didn't want to take care of me because it was a complicated case and he called headquarters in Berlin. There was a general on duty and he called the hospital and said take him anyway. And Christmas Eve, the German had one of his friends that speaks English call me and wish me a Merry Christmas.

ENOS **SLAUGHTER**

W hen you think of the tough, hustling, blood-and-guts ballplayer, Enos Slaughter comes immediately to mind. He epitomized how baseball was supposed to be played. He played for thirteen seasons with the St. Louis Cardinals. On April 11, 1954 he was traded to the New York Yankees. There is a famous photograph of him crying in front of his locker after hearing of the trade. This was my first clue that baseball management bats ninth in unswerving loyalty to franchise players.

He loved the game, but the game did not love him back. Upon retiring as a player in 1959, he managed for two years in the minors. After that, no one in baseball was interested in giving him a job.

He had a lifetime batting average of .300, and played the game like a champion. But it took until 1985, twenty-one years after becoming eligible, for him to be inducted into the Hall of Fame.

Fair comes once a year.

I came at the tail end of the Gas House Gang. I wish I could have been with them, because I played the type of ball they were playing.

When I first went to the Cardinals, we struggled and didn't draw many people . . . 350,000 to 400,000 was a lot of people for us to draw back in the late '30s and early '40s.

October 14, 1946, the seventh game of the World Series between the Red Sox and the Cardinals, is a famous game in World Series history. The score was tied 3-3, bottom of the eighth. You led off with a single. Boston got the next two men. Harry Walker then hit

*a "Texas Leaguer" to left center. Leon Culberson fielded the ball
and you scored from first.*

A lot of people don't quite understand the situation. Earlier, Mike
Gonzalez had stopped me at third on a bad relay and we'd lost
the ball game. So, Eddie Dyer [manager] said to me, "From now
on, if you think you've got a chance to score, you go ahead and
gamble and I'll be responsible." So on this play I got a good jump
on the ball and Walker hits this ball into left center and when I
hit second, I said to myself, "I can score." And I never hesitated
from then on. All I was thinking about was maybe Roy Partee was
going to block the plate on me. I still uphold Pesky 'cause he had
his back to the infield. I think with word of mouth maybe Pesky
could have thrown me out. But he turned towards first, saw me,
then turned and throwed home and Walker goes in to second.

I blame word of mouth for not letting him know what to do
with the ball. If he'd got the ball and turned to the left and
throwed home he probably had a good chance of throwing me
out. When he turned to the right and saw me at the bend, he
throwed off balance and didn't get anything on the ball. Doerr
at second and Higgins at third, they see me running and they
should have [told] Pesky what to do with the ball.

On April 11, 1954, you were traded to the New York Yankees.

It hurt very deeply at the time. My contract was the first one
that Mr. Busch signed on December 28, 1953. He says, "You're a
credit to the game. You'll always be with me." And then four
months later, I'm in New York. I found out what a cold-hearted
game it was when they got rid of me.

I was a diehard Cardinal and I'd gave them everything I had
in baseball. I played wounded, I played every way in the world
to try to help them win. To this day I still hold it against the
Cardinal organization. I tried to get a job in baseball after I retired
and they never offered me a job as even a wash boy or scrub
boy. They never attempted to give me anything.

[When I played] the boys had more pride in their work, pride
in the uniform they wore. They went out there and did the job

like it was supposed to be done. Every ballplayer that went out wanted to win, which I don't see today. They're making so much money today I don't think a World Series ring means anything to half of 'em because what's a week's work? $75,000. When we played, you were lucky to get $5,000 after the World Series.

In 1949 I had my greatest year. I hit .336. I was leading the league with about two or three weeks to go when Jackie Robinson ended up hitting .342 and Musial .338. The St. Louis paper kind of irritated me. They said the Cardinals lost the pennant [because] Slaughter run out of gas. I hit .336. I didn't hear them say a thing about Musial running out of gas.

I played ball like it should be played. I played for the win. I don't think that I got the recognition that ballplayers are getting today, and don't even hit but .250.

I did everything Casey Stengel would want me to do. I wasn't playing much and I went to Casey and I said, "Casey, I'd like to play more." He says, "You play when I want you to play and you'll be around a long time." So I kept my mouth shut. When he wanted me to play, I played. When he wanted a pinch hitter, I'd go up and pinch-hit and do everything I could to help the Yankees win.

The Athletics moved to Kansas City in '55; Johnny Sain and I were sold to Kansas City. I go over there and had a great year. The Yankees got in trouble and needed a left-hand hitter, so they bought me back in August '56. I go over and help them win the pennant. Then in the World Series, I played in Don Larsen's perfect game and the Dodgers had us two games to nothin' and I hit a three-run homer to put us back on the track. We won in seven games and I hit .350 in the World Series.

September 5, 1959, I got hit with a foul tip off my own bat. I stayed in New York and took treatments and nobody x-rayed my foot. Casey called me in and he says, "I'm trying to help you get into another World Series." Wes Covington of Milwaukee had busted a knee and they needed a left-hand hitter. I says, "Casey, you know I can't play." He says, "Well, go in and talk to Mr.

Weiss," and I did and he called John McHale of Milwaukee and I told him that I couldn't run. But he says, "If you can pinch-hit, join us." So I joined them the next day and I played the last two weeks and we finished in a tie and the Dodgers beat us in the play-offs, so I came home. And the third metatarsal's broken in my foot. Nobody knew I had a broken foot.

Marty Marion and Milt Fishman, an insurance man in St. Louis, was trying to get the franchise in Houston. They worked a deal with the American Association. They had the franchise there for the minor league club and they had a working agreement with the Chicago Cubs. I sent Ron Santo and Billy Williams to the big leagues. I had a team [Houston] that finished third, and got beat in the seventh game of the play-offs for the championship, and I can't get a job in '61.

Herb Brett had a team in Raleigh. The Mets had been accepted in the big leagues and they wanted to start a minor league organization. He finally got the Mets to let me manage Raleigh in the Carolina League, in Class B. I run fifty-four players through there that year and they told me to do the best I could. They'd take care of me. Well, they did. We finished on the bottom and I haven't been in baseball since.

I don't blame the players for getting all they can. When they threw the reserve clause out of baseball they killed baseball. We started a pension plan and the players today don't care anything for the players that [started it]. We all got shortchanged on the pension.

I'm getting about $2,100 a month. Twenty-two years in the big leagues. When it first started we paid out of our pocket. Then in '52 everybody paid $344 a year into it and the club matched it. Then when television come in everything went boomin' and how much money they're getting into it today I don't know, but it's up in the millions.

I wouldn't trade the era I played in for nothin', 'cause we had pride in ourselves, and we had pride in the teams that we represented on the field. Players today become free agents. Whoever's running the arbitration, they don't know what the heck a ballplayer's like. I don't think they know a ballplayer from an orange or a lemon. To give them such money.

I got my records in the book to show what I did. I don't have to take a back seat to anybody going into Cooperstown and the Hall of Fame. My record's there. I know the writers never did see fit and then the Veterans Committee; I played in the big leagues before quite a few of these Veterans Committee [members] even come into baseball. I had to raise all kind of hell to get in. I can't see it. Today, if somebody come along and hit a few home runs and hit .250, they go in on the first ballot. It don't make sense. It's a popularity contest.

HAL **NEWHOUSER**

al was labeled a "war-time pitcher," someone who compiled his record pitching against inferior competition during World War II. This reputation greatly delayed his induction into the Hall of Fame.

His lifetime record was 207-150. During the war, from 1942-1945, he was 70-49, a .588 percentage. From 1946 to the end of his career in 1955, he was 119-80, a .598 percentage. This tells the tale: he was a consistent quality pitcher irrespective of the era.

It took over thirty years to accomplish, but on August 2, 1992, he was inducted into the Hall of Fame. Regardless how long it took, Hal Newhouser was always a Hall of Famer.

In the fall of 1943, I graduated from high school, a trade school, as a drafting engineer. My dad was working at Chrysler. He was a draftsman. Because of a relative working with Chrysler, they were allowed to have their family come in and get a job and learn a trade from Chrysler. Because I was playing ball I had to get away from machinery because it could hurt my hand. So I took up drafting. I liked it. With the help of my dad I was coming along pretty good. With the four really bad seasons I had with Detroit I was quite demoralized and down on myself. The salary I was making in baseball, I could make that or more in the drafting field. I got married, we had our first child and I said, "Why should I put the family through all this aggravation, going down to spring training and going through this whole thing again?"

I made up my mind to [either] stay with Chrysler Corporation as a draftsman and give up baseball, or go down with a different attitude in the spring of 1944 and just say to myself, *I'm going to give it one more year and take a leave of absence from Chrysler.* My wife, who always backed me, thought it was a good plan because she always felt I should be in baseball because it was in my blood. In the interim, Detroit hired a fellow by the name of Paul Richards. He was a manager at Atlanta with their AAA club and they brought him up to catch me.

I didn't realize at the time that the Tigers set me up with Paul Richards. No matter where I went, there was Paul Richards to catch me. I'd go out to pitch batting practice and there would be Paul Richards behind the plate. The spring training games started. I would pitch, there would be Paul Richards. He'd come out to the mound say, "Hal, I can help you if you want some help. You gotta watch your temperament a little bit. Don't argue with the umpire. Let me do that. That's my job."

All of a sudden things became a little easier. The start of the 1944 season, I didn't start off that good. Then I relieved in Cleveland and I pitched the last three innings and everything came together. I strung out about nine wins in a row and lost one. I won eight in a row and lost one. Won nine in a row and lost one. It got to a point where I could go into my windup, and Paul hasn't given me a signal yet, and I already knew what he was going to ask for. Paul being very, very quiet and me being highstrung and listening to him became a real nice package.

We lost the last day of the [1944] season for the pennant. The next year we went down to spring training and Paul said, "Hal, you had a good year. The boys are in the service. You know they're going to start pickin' on you now. They're going to say that you pitched during the war and the DiMaggios and the Williamses and the Charlie Kellers' are in the service. You've got to accept this because you're going to have the media asking why did you have four [bad[seasons in a row, then all of a sudden you win? Is it because the guys are in the service?" I began to absorb what Paul was saying. I could feel it coming. And sure enough, every town I'd go into I'd be asked the same question —"How come you turned around?"

Well, deciding I was going to give it one more year with a different attitude and finding a catcher like Paul Richards was the reason the whole thing turned around.

The boys came back in 1946, all the players were back. They started to come back in the middle of '45: Hank Greenberg and Virgil Trucks came out of the service. Now 1946 became a very challenging year for me because imbedded in my mind [was]: *Am I that kind of pitcher? Am I going to be that kind of pitcher in '46 when the boys are back?* I know the media is going to say, "Well, the boys are all back, what are you going to do?" So I worked extra hard. Paul Richards had left the club. Now I'm on my own, I know what I'm doing. I had a good sense of what pitching is. My control came around. I developed an excellent change of pace along with my curve ball and fast ball. Everything became easy. Probably the best year I had was 1946. The most rewarding year, even though we won the pennant and the world championship in '45. Personally, 1946 was to show the baseball world that I could pitch against anybody, at any time, at any place. If you'll look at the numbers of innings pitched, strikeouts, earned run average, you'll see that it was actually better than during the war years [26-9, 1.94 ERA, 292 innings pitched, 29 complete games and 275 strikeouts].

Now all the big boys are back. I would have led the league, but Bob Feller struck out 348. It showed me I could pitch in the big leagues. Then I had a letdown in '47. I only won seventeen and then I came back and won twenty-one and then I hurt my arm and my career was over. Even though I went on three or four more years my pitching years were over when I was 29 years old.

I hurt it in the fall of '49 and then I aggravated it in '50. We didn't know what rotor cuffs were in those days. We didn't have [the] trainers, the doctors we have nowadays to repair things. Things went along and in 1954, Hank Greenberg, who was a great friend of mine and my teammate with Detroit, was the general manager of Cleveland and called me and said, "Hal, can you do anything, because I think we've got a club over here that can win the pennant. We've got a great outfield with Doby and we've got Rosen at third and we've got Avila and we've got a great pitching staff. We've got Feller, Lemon, Wynn, Garcia, Art Houtteman. We've got two young kids—Mossi and Narleski—coming up from Tulsa. But we don't have any left-handed pitching outside of Mossi. Can you get yourself in shape? Maybe you can help us out."

My wife used to say to me, "Well, Harold, you still have it in your blood. Your arm really that bad?" So I called up Greenberg and said, "Hank, I'm going to come down there unsigned. Let me see what I can do. Let me train by myself. Don't depend on me to do anything and let me see what I can do." He said, "Fine. Lopez will let you do anything you want." [Al] Lopez turned out to be the best manager I ever played for.

I worked out in Tucson for a couple of months. Finally, Lopez came to me and he says, "Hal, spring training's going to be breaking. We've gotta find out what you can do." I said, "What clubs are coming up in spring training." He named a few. I said, "Well, I don't know too much about the National League. What is the toughest club?" He says, "Well, you've got the Giants, Willie Mays and company coming in." And I says, "All right, I'll pitch against them." "Well," he said, "I don't think that's too good of an idea because it's going to be a packed house and they're getting ready to break spring training and that's really going to force you right to the nth degree. You're coming along so well you could really get yourself hurt." I said, "No, let's find out if I can do anything once and for all. Let me pitch against the big boys."

I pitched three innings and I didn't have any problems whatsoever with Mays and company. Therefore, it put a solid foundation in Greenberg's, Lopez's and my mind that I could pitch at least three innings.

So, my last year I won seven games and lost two and I saved seven games. We won the pennant and I was very satisfied.

Greenberg asked me to come back for one more year until Herb Score was ready. When Herb Score entered the picture, you could see a boy that may have been in the Hall of Fame. He was such a fine, fine boy and he had such great ability. You didn't know whether he was going to strike out fifteen, sixteen or seventeen, or pitch a no-hitter. I knew my time was coming to an end, so June fifteenth, when the cut-down date for twenty-five players came, I retired from baseball.

The 1945 World Series between the Cubs and Detroit has been much maligned. Warren Brown, a columnist in Chicago, was asked who was going to win and he said, "Neither team is capable of winning."

I took 16-millimeter film and turned it into tape and every once in a while people come over and I run it. Some of it is very, very comical. But while we were playing the game it wasn't comical at all.

We had some things happen that [the] writers thought wasn't good. We had Hostetler at second base which was the winning run. The ball was hit to the outfield and he turned third base and Steve O'Neill, our manager, was trying to hold him up and he kept running. He got about halfway between home and third and all of a sudden he remembered, "Hey, wait a minute. He doesn't want me to go in," and he fell flat on his face and the catcher walks over and tags him out. That isn't what you would call good baseball.

Trout came in to relieve in the twelfth inning. They had a man on first base and Hack hit a ball between third and short. Greenberg is in left field and the next thing you know the ball is over Greenberg's shoulder and the winning run scored. Of course, they gave Greenberg an error on it. We found out it hit a water sprinkler. When it hit the water sprinkler, it bounced over his left shoulder. Everybody thought that's a joke. Here is a great big league ball player letting that happen.

Andy Pafko playing center field was pretty shrewd. He had the ivy out there and we were on the march to scoring some runs. I believe Cullenbine hit a ball out over his head and it ended up in the ivy. From the bench I could see the ball hung up in the ivy and he's pretending he can't find it. So it ended up a ground rule double which cost us a run. That didn't go over with the press too well.

In the seventh game I was pitching and a normal fly ball goes out to right center and Cullenbine's playing right and Doc Cramer is playing center. It's an easy out. Just a little fly ball that a Little Leaguer can catch. It dropped between them and of course that didn't go over with the press.

It was shabby at times. But you take those four plays away, it was two pretty good teams. Cavarretta was a pretty good hitter and Pafko was a good player and they had some good solid players.

But as I look at it now and rerun it I grin. To see Hostetler on the ground. To see the ball drop between the outfielders. Pafko trying to find the ball. The ball over Greenberg's shoulder. Kids come over and I run the tape for them—they laugh like the dickens. But, you know, it's not funny at the time.

The writers game me the title "War-Time Pitcher." That stayed with me. You have to wait five years to be eligible for the writers to vote on you. So now I become eligible. I think I got four votes. I could not believe it. To find out I only received out of 300-and-some votes, four—I don't know, maybe it was even two. I knew then that the writers were not going to put me into the Hall of Fame. That meant fifteen years waiting for them to vote on me.

You wait five years to be eligible. Then you're fifteen years with the writers. That's twenty years. Now when you're through with the writers, or vice versa, you've gotta wait another five years to be eligible for the Veterans Committee. Now, I'm at twenty-five years. It took six years for the Veterans Committee to decide that I belong in the Hall of Fame and there's thirty-one years.

Did it hurt? Yes. I thought it was unfortunate that the title of "War-Time Pitcher" was passed on from one writer to another as the older writers retired. The new writers that came in had never seen Hal Newhouser pitch. They'd look back in the records, they'd see "War-Time Pitcher." He won twenty-nine and twenty-five during the war, therefore, he shouldn't be eligible. Those writers went on to other jobs or they retired, and then you have your new writers coming in.

When I became eligible for the Veterans Committee there were writers like Shirley Povich from the *Washington Post* and Bob Broeg who writes for the St. Louis paper and Jack Brickhouse, on the committee out of Chicago. They had seen me play. Then fellows like Stan Musial, Ted Williams and Al Lopez. Some of them had seen me play during and after the war. It took six more years. It didn't happen overnight. They went back and looked at what I did after the war, not during the war, and that's what put me in the Hall of Fame.

For thirty-one years my wife heard me say after the announcement is made, "Well, I guess we gotta wait another year." You hear that for thirty-one years . . . that gets a little tiresome. My wife is such a super person and she understood and would console me. "Well, Harold, don't give up." Well, I'm the type of person who never gives up. You give me a challenge and I'll give you a fight for your money.

I knew they were voting on March seventeenth [1991]. I came downstairs and the wife said to me, very politely, "Well, Harold, the news really isn't all that good." I nonchalantly had my glass of juice and was having a cup of coffee and she said, "It's on the second page." It said, "Eligible for the Veterans Hall of Fame today," and named Joe Gordon, Nellie Fox, Phil Rizzuto and so on and my name wasn't even mentioned. So I just said, "Well, another year's gone by and it doesn't look like it's gonna happen now."

I'm upstairs in my room and I was doing some paperwork and it was about three o'clock and the phone rang. I said, "Hello." He said, "My name is so-and-so, I'm with the *Tampa Tribune*. Congratulations." I was taken back and I says, "Congratulations on what?" He said, "You've just been put in the Hall of Fame." I said, "I've heard that before. I've had no confirmation at all from anybody from the Hall of Fame." He says, "Well, you can rest assured that you're in. You went in on the first ballot." I said, "I haven't heard anything." He said, "I'd like to have a statement from you." I said, "I'll give you a statement, but I haven't heard anything official."

So the next thing I know all the TV stations are calling. Everybody is calling me on the phone. I still hadn't heard anything, officially. About six o'clock that night the phone rang and it was Ernie Harwell who broadcasts for the Detroit Tigers and Ernie's on the committee. He said, "Hal, we've been trying to get a hold of you. Your phone's been blocked up. I want to make it official: You are in the Hall of Fame." So I learned that I was really officially in by six o'clock that evening.

I fulfilled all my dreams for baseball. First thing I wanted to do was sign a contract with the Detroit Tigers. Later I wanted to win twenty games. Then I thought, wouldn't it be nice if I could play on an All-Star team and I did that. Then I set my sights [on] the Most Valuable Player Award. Well, I won it twice in a row. No pitcher in the history of baseball has ever done (that). Then I said maybe there's a chance I'll be in the Hall of Fame.

So all the goals, all the years I put in came together on the second of August of 1992, when the Commissioner of Baseball gave me the plaque and announced I was in the Hall of Fame. So, 8/2/92 will be remembered forever as the most exciting thing a person could ever go through. Especially my mother, to see her son placed in the Hall of Fame. And my family, my wife and everybody who kept hearing me saying, "We'll have to wait another year," won't have to hear that anymore.

ROCKY **BRIDGES**

R ocky has devoted his life to baseball. He came up to Brooklyn in 1951 and played for a total of seven teams in the majors over eleven seasons. He has managed in the minors and coached in the majors. While managing Tucson the team had a pre-game cow milking contest. He finished second and said, "I didn't try too hard. I was afraid I'd get emotionally involved with the cow."

You have been in baseball your whole life. Who are some of the more interesting people you have met?

Piersall would have to be one. He's about three blocks from the funny farm, but if it's the funny farm, it's a rich one because he's made a lot of money out of being nutty.

I was a coach when he joined the Angels. He joined us in Boston and after the first pitch—it was called a strike—he went bananas on the umpire. Maybe he had something to do at home while he was in Boston, because he left the scene after one strike. He started jumping up and down and raising hell with the umpire and before you know it he was out of the game.

He was smart like a fox. He capitalized on his goofiness which a lot of guys had done in the past. He was a superb outfielder, though.

Art Fowler was a humorous guy. He hung around Billy Martin for a long time; they were complete opposites. Art was very humorous, so was Clint Courtney in his own way. Jackie Brown, who was the pitching coach for the White Sox told a story that he was pitching in Texas and Billy Martin was managing the club. He said Art came out to him one day and said, "You know you're making Billy *awfully* mad," and he turned around and went back [to the dugout].

Clint Courtney wasn't afraid to mix it up, was a very fierce competitor, and got the most out of his ability. He couldn't understand when we told him one time that the runner on second was looking in on his signs. He said, "Naw, they don't do that." I said, "Yes, they do." And, even though he could figure out the square root of anything, those fingers, when he put them down, sometimes confused him. Many times he looked at his own fingers to make sure what sign he was putting down. After we told him they *did* look in and try to get the signs, he said, "Well, I'll give the signs when they aren't looking."

Billy Loes was a young man that came up and had a great faculty of knowing how to pitch, even at an early age when he joined Brooklyn. He could paint the plate pretty good. I guess it was in the '52 series that he said he lost a ground ball in the sun at Ebbets Field. I know he hurt his thumb one time, so he couldn't pitch, and someone asked him, "Aren't you going to do your running?" And he says, "No, running hurts my thumb."

That was a great Brooklyn team.

An outstanding team. You're looking at guys like Reese, Robinson, Hodges, Campanella, Duke Snider, Pafko. There were some great players there. It was good defensive club. Billy Cox, at that time, was the best third baseman in the National League by a long shot. He liked to hold the ball—an outstanding arm— and he gave you some heartbeats waiting to throw it to first, but he was very accurate. He was just an outstanding third baseman.

I was fortunate to play for some very fine managers, like Charlie Dressen. I thought he was a wonderful person. The two years I was there [Brooklyn], he was there. I enjoyed him a lot. My favorite manager was Birdie Tebbetts. I was with him about three years, and as far as knowledge of the game, he was one of the best I've been around.

Had I been playing now I would have loved to play for Jimmy Leyland. In Leyland's case he had eighteen years in the minors.

He didn't play in the big leagues. He appreciates everything that has happened to him. Birdie did play in the major leagues, but their psychology with players is just outstanding. Who to pat on the back and who to kick in the rump. There's an old saying, "most of the time its only six inches from a pat on the back or a kick in the ass."

I had a girl moon me in Tucson. This guy that was a stockholder in the Tucson club was a character. He was always trying to pull some stuff and a lot of times it was on me because I would go along with the joke. He had a gal parachute in a bikini and land at home plate with a lineup card.

I was coaching third and here comes a gal strolling out toward me. She said, "Hi, Rocky" and then bent over and flipped her skirt up—she had a G-string on, but it was a bare asset she was showing.

He had a gal come out like she was pregnant, saying, ""Rocky, Rocky!" I said, "Oh, no, no, no—the devil made me do it." Right in back of her was a TV camera.

Baseball's different today. Not just the money; everybody talks about the money. But, heck, if the guys can get more, more power to them. Everybody knows you're not worth the money they're paying.

You've got better conditions, fields, stuff like that. The traveling is quicker. But I think they've lost some of the comradeship we had. They get on airplanes and they sit two seats [away] unless they really like each other. Then you get to the hotel and [they] usually all have separate rooms. When I first started playing, you rode trains, you got to know each other a lot better. They've gone from beer drinkers to cocktail drinkers. Obviously, some of them went to worse things than that.

We had more pride. You played hard and if you weren't doing the best you could the guys on the team would hop [on] you. I don't think that happens much anymore.

CAL **ABRAMS**

His dream growing up in Brooklyn was to play for the Dodgers. It came true in 1949. It would not take long for Cal to go down in Dodger history.

On October 1, 1950, the Phillies were playing the Dodgers at Ebbets Field. It was the last game of the season and Philadelphia was one game up on Brooklyn. If the Dodgers won there would be a play-off for the pennant. The game was 1-1 in the Dodger half of the ninth. Cal led off with a walk, Pee Wee Reese singled to left, Abrams stopping at second. Duke Snider hit Robin Roberts' first pitch into center and Cal was off. Milt Stock, the Dodger third base coach, waived Cal home. Richie Ashburn's throw nailed him by at least fifteen feet. Roberts retired the next two batters. In the top of the tenth Dick Sisler hit a three-run home run. The Dodgers did not score in the bottom of the tenth, and the Phillies won 4-1, taking the National League pennant.

My early days in Brooklyn were very pleasant. Being a hometown boy, playing with Brooklyn was the dream of every young kid that went to school in Brooklyn. I was no exception. In 1950 I had a good spring training. Unfortunately, there's always thirteen outfielders trying out for left field. Right and center were always taken. Naturally, Duke Snider and Carl Furillo had those sewed up.

Mr. Rickey kept sending me down to the minors, promising to get me back because he wanted a good Jewish outfielder. And being from Brooklyn would be an asset, too. So I went back to Mobile, to Fort Worth, to St. Paul in three options. In 1950 things didn't turn out the way I wanted them to. I thought I was going to get the leadoff spot, but I didn't.

Mr. Rickey was a very shrewd businessman. He had a heart of gold, but he knew how to hide it. My first salary was $75 a month. I often wonder would any of these ballplayers making $24 million play for $75 a month in the minors.

The minimum in Brooklyn was $5,000. That's what I received in '50. But up until '49, I was getting [a] minor league salary. Even $5,000 for six months was really nothing, but I was a happy-go-lucky kid. I was on cloud nine and nobody could disturb me. They would say, "You Jew SOB," I would say something funny. For example, I was hitting .477 July 15, 1951. Batting champion of both leagues. Some guy in Cincinnati yelled over, "You Jew SOB. I wish I had your nose full of nickels." I yelled back as I led off, "I wish I had it full of pennies and I would be very happy. I'd be a millionaire." And then [I] go and get a base hit which really put the icing on top.

We had one utility infielder—I won't mention his name—but one day he called me a Bolshevik and Charlie Dressen came running out and said to him, "If I ever hear you say anything detrimental again you'll be back in the farm system if you're playing at all." I turned to him and said, "You know, you don't even know what a Bolshevik is. You're Polish. You don't know nothing."

Coming out of Ebbets Field we had these wonderful kids that idolized us and they had penny postcards. Every single day this one kid always jumped in front of everybody. "Could I have your autograph?" with these penny postcards. So after three weeks of signing for him, we were going on a road trip, I asked him, "I have to ask you something. Why do you need so many autographs?" He said, "Cal, I need twenty-one Cal Abrams to trade for one Carl Furillo."

The Dodger Knothole Gang with Happy Felton. You take three youngsters in the outfield, you play with them and pick one. That one person is allowed to go into the dugout to talk to any of the Dodgers he wanted prior to the game. Playing with them in the outfield and talking with them in the dugout, the Dodgers

received $50 from the TV program. I had not been on the pro-
gram for an entire year. The last week of the season, Happy
Felton came over and said, "All right, Cal, you're on." I was really
angry to tell you the truth, because Jackie Robinson was on fifty
times, so that's $2,500. Well, anyway, I went to the outfield and
these three boys were there and I approached one and I said,
"Listen," whispering in his ear, "I'm going to pick you. Now I'll
get $50 for that. Then when they ask you who you want to talk
to in the dugout, you say you want to talk to me. That gives me
$100." So I was playing with them and finally Happy Felton said,
"Who's the best." I said, "Oh, Happy, this fellow here. What a pair
of hands. Great glove man." "Congratulations, son, who would
you like to talk to." He says, "Carl Furillo."

I roomed with Chuck Conners, the Rifleman. He played with
me in Mobile, Alabama, and he had a cup of coffee with the
Dodgers. We always got bedchecked at midnight by the clubhouse
trainer who would come to your door, knock, and have this big
board in front of him. I opened the door sleepily and he said, "Hi,
Cal, any candy in the room?" I said, "What are you talking about?
We're sleeping." Meanwhile, he's checking my name off on the
board. He says, "Is Chuck in there?" I said, "Of course he is." He
says, "Do you mind if I come in and look?" I said, "No." He comes
in, sees him, he puts a checkmark. The next night the same thing,
he knocks on the door, "Hi, Cal, any candy?" I say, "No, what are
you doing here? You're waking me." He says, "That's all right." He
marks me off. "Is Chuck in there?" I say, "Yes, dammit, come on."
He comes in. Checks him off. The third night, Chuck says to me,
"I'm sneaking out, Cal, and I want you to take care of it for me."
I say, "What are you talking about? How can I take care of anything for you?" He says, "You're Jewish, you got a good mind,
you'll figure out something." John, the trainer, came up, knocked
on the door. "Hi, Cal." he checks me off. "Any candy?" "No." "Is
Chuck in?" I grabbed him by the arm, I says, "For God's sake.
Three nights in a row. Come here." I grabbed him by the arm and
I started yanking him in the room and he stopped and pulled back.
"Yeah, I believe you." He checked him off. I got away with it.

You are playing the Phillies at Ebbets Field on October 1, 1950. If the Dodgers beat them they will tie for the National League lead and force a play-off. It's the bottom of the ninth and you are on second base with no outs. The score is 1-1.

Man on first and second, nobody out and I'm the winning run. Robin Roberts is pitching, Stan Lopata is catching. Lopata gives Robin Roberts a pick-off sign to get me at second base. Richie Ashburn saw the sign and he immediately started to charge in behind second base in case Roberts threw wild to second base; he could stop the ball and prevent me from going to third. Roberts was nervous. Duke Snider our home run hitter was up [but Roberts] missed the sign. Instead he fired the ball home. Snider hit a line drive right by me. I knew it was a base hit. I knew if everyone were playing where they were supposed to be I would win the game for the club. I started running as hard as I could to third base. Milton Stock, our coach, was waving [me] home frantically. He didn't see where Ashburn was, but then his eyes traveled back toward second—he saw Ashburn had already thrown the ball home as I was just touching third base—full speed. I noticed that he had one hand in his mouth biting [his] nails, and the other hand still waving me home. When I rounded third, Lopata was fifteen to twenty-five feet up the base-line with the ball in his glove. Running full force, there was no way for me to stop and get back. So the only thing that I could do was try to run into him. He killed me because he had on all that paraphernalia. I was out. Carl Furillo popped a foul for the second out. Gil Hodges hit a long fly ball that was caught for the third out.

The next inning Dick Sisler hit a home run over my head. We couldn't catch them in our half. They fired Milton Stock the following day for sending me home. However, he told the newspaper people that if he had it to do over again he would do it exactly the same way.

Some of the newspaper people had written, "Cal was leaning backwards when the ball was hit. Cal took a wide turn around third base. Cal didn't get a good jump on the ball." So on and so forth. So they made me the goat, basically. However, two years later, this story came out [Roberts missing the sign] in *Sport Magazine* and I was very relieved that I was no longer the goat.

The next year Bobby Thomson hit the home run to beat you.

Andy Pafko was playing left field at the time. Thomson hit the home run off of Ralph Branca, and the game was over. I don't remember walking across the Polo Grounds into our clubhouse. I floated across, I think. The next thing I remembered I was in the clubhouse. I don't remember ever leaving the dugout.

When the manager called the bullpen for a relief pitcher, he yelled to Clyde Sukeforth, the bullpen coach, "Hurry up and get two guys warmed up. Quick. Quick." Branca and Labine started throwing hard. Branca was throwing hard fastballs. The manager called back and said, "Who's throwing the hardest?" Clyde looked and Branca had just thrown a hard fastball and Labine had thrown a curve, a beautiful curve that bounced in the dirt. Clyde said, "Well, Branca's throwing hard." And he brought him in. Bobby Thomson had hit five home runs in the course of the year off of Branca, so he was at ease at the plate. Branca coming in was saying, "He hit five home runs off of me." He wasn't at ease going to the pitcher's mound. There was a big difference there. Bobby Thomson felt much better at the plate than Branca did on the mound.

Charlie Dressen never said "boo" to me. He never said I did well. Never said "good throw," or this or that. I later found out that he was anti-Semitic. I hit .477 and we were on the road and came back to Brooklyn. I had been playing every day, leading off. There was absolutely nothing wrong with me. Something made me look at the lineup as we were about to run out to our positions. I had over one hundred relatives and friends in the stands. I wasn't leading off. I sat on one end of the bench and Dressen was on the other end of the bench. In my day, you don't go over to the manager, punch him in the nose and say, "You SOB, why ain't I playing?" Today it's a different story. You go and punch him, get fined $10,000, write out a check and you're there.

In our day you never said "boo," especially if you were Jewish. He didn't want a Jewish ballplayer leading the league.

I recall one time at the end of the season Charlie Dressen told us, "I do not want any of you going to the racetracks, talking to touts or gamblers," so on and so forth. When we got home after the season I picked up the *Sporting News* and there he is putting a wreath on a horse at Santa Anita. So, I cut out the clipping and waited 'til spring training. When we went in that year I ran into his office while he was taking a shower and put the clipping on his table. He came running out and wanted to know who did it. Of course I'm not going to say "me" because that's the end of my career. But, you know, "Do as I say, but don't do as I do."

You were traded to Cincinnati in June 1952.

The trade was a quick thing. We were in Cincinnati for three games. I had played the first two games with the Dodgers and the third day I put my Dodger uniform on, somebody tapped me on the shoulder and said, "Take it off. We just traded you to Cincinnati."

But a very wonderful thing happened that afternoon and I got a glowing look from Jackie Robinson that made me feel that I was an accomplished ballplayer. Ted Kluszewski was playing first base and I was in right field and Jackie hit a single to me. One of those shots where the ball bounces right into your glove. You got it, one-two-three. I said to myself, "Being as I'm not in Brooklyn anymore, I don't give a damn. If I make errors I don't care." So I whipped the ball as hard as I could right to Ted Kluszewski at first. I knew Jackie would race around the base, stop on a dime and if you juggled the ball continue running to second. But when he stopped on a dime, my ball went like a bullet and hit Teddy right in the middle of the stomach. I threw it as hard as I could. That ball rolled off of him like it was a ping pong ball. It didn't even faze him. The only reason he didn't catch it he was watching Jackie's foot to make sure he touched first base. Now, the ball rolled down Ted's leg and Jackie dove back into first, got up, brushed himself off, looked out at me in right field and he gave me the nicest, biggest, smile I ever saw. He was actually talking to me, I could tell. He was saying, "Cal, you're a hell of a ballplayer."

Lon Warneke was an old pitcher and umpire. I yelled at everybody. I yelled at the Giants. I did whatever I could to disturb and distract them. So this particular afternoon Lon Warneke comes over and he says to us and the Giants, "The first guy that opens his mouth toward the opposition, I'm going to clear out the bench." Well, I didn't like that. You know, it bothered me. So I got an idea. I stood on the steps and the Boy Scouts have their semaphore flags and the Navy has it for landing planes. I'm standing on the steps looking at the Giants and I'm waving my hands like I have flags in them. He comes running over to me and says, "You're out of the game." I said, "What are you throwing me out for? I didn't say a word." He said, "No, but I know how to spell."

Now, lightning always strikes twice. Three months later, I'm leading off and Warneke is behind the plate. I didn't mean to say anything, but this is what came out of my mouth: "Mr. Warneke, can you throw *anybody* out for thinking?" He said, "No." I said, "I think you're a son of a bitch." And he said, "Get out." The only two times in my career that I was thrown out.

I wish I had my life to live over again because I would do exactly the same thing. I was happy to be one of the boys of summer.

NED **GARVER**

D id you ever work for a company that was going nowhere? Ned Garver did—for fourteen years in the big leagues. Not only one, but four teams that never finished in the first division. Fourteen years of mediocrity and pain. He pitched 2,477⅓ innings from 1948 to 1961 in frustration.

He was a tough competitor who pitched for the St. Louis Browns from 1948 to 1952. In 1951 they finished last with a record of 52-102. Ned won twenty games, or 38% of their total victories. He is the only pitcher to win twenty games for a team that lost a hundred games.

He hurt his arm in 1952 and was never the same again. He ended his career with the Los Angeles Angels in 1961. His totals were 129-157, but with better teams and a sound arm he would have been one of the best.

From 1949 through 1951 you won forty-five games, or 28% of the Browns' total victories. You were carrying the team.

To win forty-five games in a three-year span with that ball club was quite an accomplishment. That would earn you a lot of money today.

Things were different then. I was a pretty good hitter, so they didn't take me out. I got to stay in ball games where somebody else didn't. I was young and worked at conditioning myself in the winter time. [We] played a lot of day games and it was hot in St. Louis, so if I stayed strong I could win ball games by being a good hitter, getting to stay in ball games. I tied the league in complete games in 1950 and led in 1951.

The last nineteen games I started in 1950, the only time I was taken out was when Cal Hubbard [umpire] came out and I was sick. He called Zack Taylor [manager] out and told him I hadn't ought to be out there so they took me out of the ball game. But that was the only game that I went out of in the last nineteen and then the next year, 1951, I completed twenty-four of the thirty games I started.

I felt the players had confidence in me in that if they would get me a run or two I might be able to hold it. I always told the boys, "Don't worry about an error." Everybody makes an error. I got to play regularly and I didn't spend a lot of time feeling sorry for myself that I was with the Browns. A lot of clubs were showing interest in me. The Red Sox were offering a lot of money and the Yankees offering a bunch of players. I was smart enough not to worry about things that I didn't have any control over.

I wasn't worrying about the guys playing behind me. I had my own job. As a result of the financial situation in St. Louis they had to sell ballplayers. They would sell players and trade 'em and get young guys. So we had people playing out of position. We had people playing in the big leagues with a limited amount of experience and we had some promising folks. But it was going to take a while for them to develop.

Things were tough back in those years because you only had eight major league clubs. The Yankees had a couple of ball clubs over there; the team sitting on the bench could win. They had two men at every position. The Red Sox had a super ball club. And the Indians. There were a lot of good people.

You have a lot of good players now but you have too many teams. So you end up with some people who should be in the minor leagues, but aren't. Back in those days we had some people playing for us that probably should have been in the minor leagues. But we had some good talent. We had Dillinger and Zarilla and Jerry Priddy. We had some people that could play, but in 1947 they'd gotten rid of guys like Galehouse and Kramer and Vern Stephens to Boston. You get rid of three people like that, two of them off your pitching staff, and Stephens went over there and knocked in 159 runs.

I think the Browns would be as good or better as these expansion teams. I was in an expansion club, too. When the league expanded I went to the Los Angeles Angels.

As soon as it was established that they weren't going to do much with their veteran players who were making a reasonable amount of money, they got rid of those high priced guys making about $25 to $28,000. Now, the minimum's about $109,000.

Bill Veeck gave me a contract saying I'd make an extra $5,000 if they drew 500,000 people, but they didn't come close. We drew more people in Cleveland in 1948 as the visiting team [11 games] than we did in St. Louis [for 77 games].

I opened the season in 1949—I've got the article—against Bob Feller, and they were the world champions. We opened in St. Louis and drew 12,000 and some people. I think I've got that sucker . . . here it is.

"The Indians lost to the upstart St. Louis Browns 5-1. Ned Garver scattered 7 hits to beat the champs before 12,817 people, the Browns' largest opening crowd in 15 years."

There was a New York writer named John Lardner who wrote, "Bill Veeck bought the St. Louis Browns under the impression that the Browns were owned."

He was the greatest. I loved Bill Veeck. Most every player did. He was something else. You knew that he might trade you next week, but as long as you played for him he made you feel you were ten feet tall.

He was close to you. He'd talk to you like you were one of the guys. If you came up to the office to get your mail or something, he'd holler at you and have you come in. Sometimes he'd come down and pitch batting practice to the pitchers. He was down to earth and friendly and so consistent, nothing phony about him.

He wanted to be fair with you. If they were going to do halfway well, he wanted you to be in on it.

First year I was in the big leagues they made me sign a contract for $3,500. The most I made playing for the Browns was the contract I signed for Veeck. That was $25,000 [1951].

You were traded on August 14, 1952, to the Detroit Tigers.

I wasn't glad to be traded. That's kind of a sad feeling. You're part of that team. You're part of that organization. You feel a great degree of loyalty. Like going to your high school or something. You develop a considerable amount of love and affection for that organization, and they had been the ball club that had given me the chance to play in the first place. They signed me. Let me play in their minor league system and eventually got to the big leagues. Well, if nobody would have done that I'd have been a farmer. Been milking cows. When I heard that I was traded makes you feel they don't like you any more or they don't want you any more. But I liked Detroit. That was my team when I was a kid, so I was thrilled to be able to play there.

I started the '52 season in Detroit and shut 'em out. The next game I shut somebody else out. I figure if I hadn't got hurt I might have gone to Cooperstown. I was on top of my game and my confidence was good. I had good stuff and fine control and I had had three pretty good years. Now it started with two shutouts.

I'm throwing batting practice to some of the other pitchers at Sportsman's Park. It felt like somebody threw a baseball from the outfield and hit me in the back of the neck. I herniated a disc. I've had it operated on since. It came out and pressed on the nerve and affected the arm. I kept trying to pitch, which was a stupid thing. The next game, I had them shut out for about seven innings and then I just ran out of gas. Then I couldn't straighten my arm out.

It wasn't anything I did. Wasn't anything unusual. But the stupid part came when I tried to pitch a game. I couldn't straighten my arm out 'til it was time to pitch because the nerves to the arm were being affected.

I kept trying to pitch until I finally couldn't. I opened for Detroit on the fourteenth of August, pitched on the seventeenth of August and that was the last time I pitched. I took treatments all that next winter. Soaked my elbow every cussed night. Charlie Gehringer sent me to a guy that probably broke those adhesions loose and was probably responsible for my being able to come back and play the next year. I never was close to being the [same] pitcher after that, although I was able to be reasonably successful. I'd win ten to twelve games. I pitched quite a bit, but I was never close to being as good after that.

I played for four major league clubs and the only one left is the Tiger ball club. I played for the Kansas City Athletics; [now] they're the Oakland Athletics. I played for the Los Angeles Angels and now they're the California Angels. I was one of the original players out there. But they've changed their location. They've changed their name.

They're all gone. Tiger Alumni is the only . . . we have a pretty good association up there and we do a lot of things for charity and stuff. But the rest of the ball clubs don't have you back for old timers' games because you're not part of it.

You miss it, of course. It was so terribly important to you. Everything I did was geared to making me a successful player, especially after I got to the big leagues. When I was in the minor leagues I had to have a winter job to make a living.

I got started in something else. I had an eighteen-year career that grew into a corporate job with a meat packing company and retired from there when I was 55 years old.

Sometimes I get to thinking, I don't believe I did that. I don't believe I pitched against DiMaggio and Williams and those folks. But I know one thing, I got to play in an awful good era.

DAVID **CLYDE**

e was the number one draft pick in 1973 and the talk of base-ball. David signed with the Texas Rangers for $65,000 going directly from high school to the majors. He started eight-een games and had a record of 4-8. According to David, the Rangers used him as a drawing card, gave him no instruction, and this, cou-pled with his age, helped to send his career tumbling before it ever started. He became injured, was sent to the minors, was traded twice and finally called it quits in 1981. He had great potential, but it just did not work out. His big league record was 18-33. A teammate said, "The system chewed him up."

The good Lord blessed me with a good left arm and the abil-ity to use it. Whether you'd want to consider it the right place at the right time can be debatable, but I was fortunate to be drafted and had an opportunity to play professional baseball. I was drafted and joined the Texas Rangers the first week in June [1973] and spent the second half of the season with them.

My manager was Whitey Herzog, and Whitey was excellent for young players. Whitey developed the '69 Mets. He was director of player personnel for the Mets organization during that time and developed those players. Over the years he's been a proven winner.

I think in Whitey's mind he felt I had the physical tools to be there, but the mental aspect of the game was completely different. I think they just took it that, hey, he's here for this year and then we'll send him out and get some seasoning and start teaching him the game.

You grow up with these dreams of what big league ball's all about and you have your heroes and everything and all of a sudden you're out there one day doin' it. One minute you're on the high school field, the next minute you're playing with guys you've always dreamed about playing with. You think you have to be better than you actually are. And I guess that comes with maturity. Instead of relying on my God-given ability and the hard work that I'd put forth, I felt I can do better than this because I'm no longer facing high school hitters, I'm facing the best. So instead of throwing in the low nineties, I felt I had to throw in the high nineties. Thinkin' I had to have a better breakin' ball. Those things just compounded themselves and made for many, many frustrating evenings.

Bob Short, who owned the Rangers at the time, was in dire financial trouble as [to] whether he was going to be able to keep the ball club.

I brought him some money that first year. The Rangers drew a little over half a million people, and I was there only half a year and was responsible for drawing about 230,000 of them. So I put some money in his pocket, but he needed more than that.

The last month of the '73 season may have been the turning point in my career going downhill. That was the firing of Whitey Herzog and the hiring of Billy Martin.

Billy was the manager the following year and I got caught in a power play. Billy didn't want me there, felt that I needed to be sent out where I could pitch every fifth day and learn the trade. Billy hadn't, over the years, liked working with younger players. He always had been able to get an extra mile or two out of some guys that were considered over the hill.

Well, the ownership wanted me there to put people in the stands and I got caught in between. Billy said, "No, he's not going to be here," and therefore I'm the one who suffered. I won my first three starts in 1974 and then wasn't even allowed to throw on the side for thirty days. Everything was done to try to break me. I had lost my breakin' ball, I was trying to re-find it and wasn't really given much opportunity to work on it. And at the big league level, during a game, you can't afford to work on it. One game can cost you a shot at going to the World Series. I understand Billy's plight, but yet, in some instances I think I was sacrificed.

I lost nine straight. I never did get back in the rotation. Here I am, 19 years old, a spot-starter in the big leagues. Considered one of the best pitching prospects at the time—and they are letting me pitch every two or three weeks.

Nineteen seventy-five was my first year in the minor leagues. I spent a year at "AA," Pittsfield, Massachusetts and enjoyed that year. It was one of my most enjoyable years in professional baseball. I made some good friends. I was able to go out and pitch every fifth day. I started finding my breakin' ball again. I had a winning record in the minor leagues at that point and I was brought back up in September. I had one start against the California Angels and carried a three- or four-hit shutout into the eighth inning. And then, because of a fielding mistake on my part, cost myself an opportunity to win that ball game. I think we were winning 1 to 0. I may have given up a lead-off walk or a lead-off base hit. Mickey Rivers at bat. Mickey laid a bunt down and I threw it to the right field corner . . . at that time Mickey could fly. I threw him a triple, let's put it that way.

My first injury was in 1976. In spring training somehow I injured my arm. I was a power pitcher and every time I went to reach back for my fast ball it wasn't there. There was a dull, constant ache. I pitched in the famous Sacramento Stadium that had about a 200-foot left field fence and made it very difficult to pitch in. I pitched three or four games that year and spent the rest of the year on the disabled list with my first shoulder operation.

Next year, they've moved Sacramento to Tucson. I consider '77 a very successful season. I'm coming back from major surgery and was able to throw the ball hard and didn't experience any arm problems at all that year. I think I was 7 and 11 or something that year. But I considered it a success for the simple fact that it was my first year back from major arm surgery and I still had good velocity on the ball and was able to go out there every fifth day.

You were traded in '78 to Cleveland. You had an 8 and 11 record with a 4.28 earned run average.

Until I reached Cleveland, I had seen no one in the Ranger organization that could teach me anything about pitching. I'm not going to include Whitey or Chuck Estrada in that statement. Here I am, a 19-year-old young man who throws in the low nineties, and they're trying to make me a sinker-slider pitcher. You go back and look at the Rangers' history over the last twenty years. Look at the draft choices they've had as far as pitchers go and they have had some of the finest young arms in baseball. I'm not saying that we would have all developed into great big league pitchers, but you would have thought that out of that group of fifteen or twenty arms there would have been a few of us. They had myself, Pete Broberg, Don Stanhouse, Lenny Barker, Tommy Boggs . . . I'm talking about fifteen or twenty guys who threw 90 plus.

I thoroughly enjoyed getting away from the Texas situation and getting under somebody who was willing to work with me. The only instruction I received from my pitching coach in 1974 was, "I'll kiss your ass if they hit it, if you throw it over the plate." That's all I was told. There's nothing like, "You're rushing your body, you're dropping your elbow, you need to get on top of the ball." Nothing.

In '79 you were 3-4 with Cleveland.

Spent some time on the disabled list. I had some back problems. I didn't have any arm problems. Started the season on the disabled list with an ulcer. Then came off the disabled list and won my first two or three starts and then started having some personal problems at home that shouldn't have affected me, but I allowed it to cross over a little bit. Then spent the last month of the season on the disabled list with some back problems.

I was traded back to Texas [in 1979] and then Texas released me in spring training. I went to spring training in great shape. Everybody was complimenting me on how good a shape I was in, how well I was throwing the ball. Then the first day that I was to face live hitters, throwing battin' practice, I went out and couldn't pick my arm up. Somehow or other I'd injured my arm again and I really don't know how, where or when. I was released by Texas at the end of spring training while I was injured.

I had surgery again. I went to several shoulder specialists around the country to get several opinions. We tried conservative approaches at first and it wasn't gettin' any better. So in April '80 I was operated on again. Made another come-back in '81. I signed with the Astros organization and went to Class AA Columbus, and baseball was fun again. The Astros were one of the best organizations I played with as far as the way they treated their players. I was either 6 and 1 or 7 and 1 at Columbus and was Pitcher of the Month in the Southern League and things were fun again. I was brought up to AAA Tucson again and I never did have much success in the PCL and started having a little trouble getting my breakin' ball over.

The Astros had a lot of interest in me. They invited me to the Instructional League that year. One morning I was out on the mound about the first or second inning, taking my warmups, and all of a sudden I asked myself, "What am I doing out here?" That had never happened to me before. I loved baseball and would do anything to play it. I would have done anything. All of a sudden I am asking myself, "What am I doing out here" and right then and there I knew it was time to hang 'em up because I wasn't being fair to my teammates, I wasn't being fair to the organization, and I wasn't being fair to myself. That was in the fall of 1981.

The thing I regret, the only reason I wish I was still playing today, is for my two sons to experience what it's like to be in a big league ball park and hang around those guys.

JACKIE **WARNER**

A fter the first 15 games of his rookie season with the California Angels in 1966, he was batting .345, had 5 home runs and 13 RBIs. He then injured his hand. Jackie played hurt, his production fell off, and by July he was back in the minors.

He never got back to the majors and left baseball in 1970. He went to work as a truck driver and has been at it ever since.

I was playing against the Washington Senators and a left-handed pitcher named Pete Richert kept throwin' me fast ball sliders. I kept foulin' them off and finally he threw me a hard slider inside. I had already started my swing and I tried to adjust and it was a real freak thing. I popped the ligaments in my hand between my thumb and index finger. I played the rest of that day. It took two years to heal, mainly because I didn't get the rest I needed and the proper care.

When we came back home they injected it with cortisone for about four or five days. I kept in the lineup and it just didn't work. It was excruciating pain and whenever I'd swing and miss it was very painful. I couldn't swing right. I struck out a lot and it was a very humiliating experience.

I hurt it about the second week in May. They tried playing me and it wasn't working and finally, after Rigney [Bill Rigney, manager] seen I couldn't do it, he rested me for a while. It was July 4th when I finally got back in and we were playing the Detroit Tigers in Detroit. Mickey Lolich was pitching and my hand did get better, but it still wasn't strong. I hit a home run to straight away center field off of Lolich. From there we went to Baltimore and I got to hit off of Dave McNally and Steve Barber, a couple of lefties. I did well against them . . . the hand wasn't feeling too bad. We came back home and Rigney was just putting me in against left-handers. Dennis Bennett, I believe, was pitching that night and I lined out to third and I think I got a base hit. Then they sent me down. I never could figure that out. I went to Seattle and in batting practice I popped it again. It wasn't strong, it popped again and just the same old story. It didn't get better. I just kept playin' and that winter I had to go to work. I had financial obligations to my son. I got a job working at General Mills unloading hundred-pound sacks of flour off box cars all day long.

Before spring training I called Roland Hemond, the farm director at the time. I told him about my hand. I said, "Hey, this thing's still hurting and spring training's just around the corner." He sent me to see Dr. Kerlan. I saw him in January of '67 and he said, "Why didn't you get in to see me sooner?" I said, "Well, that was up to the Angels to do that and I guess they didn't see fit for me to see you." So he injected it with cortisone and of course prior to this I had had injections but it hadn't really done much good.

He said, "Don't do anything with it for a month." So I didn't. Then I went to spring training and it felt better for a couple of weeks and then it started again. I was getting cortisone shots. They decided to send me back down to the minors and Rigney told me, "You know, in the front office you have a reputation for being a hypochondriac." That really upset me. I said, "I don't care what the front office says or thinks or you or anyone else. This makes me angry because you don't have anybody out there that wants to play in the major leagues any more than I do. As a kid I sacrificed and I worked hard. I worked out when other kids were going to the beach and doing all those things. You answer a question for me. Why would anybody that has gone out and worked hard and busted their back and got off to a good start like I did last year, why would I want to make up something? I finally got to the major leagues. That was my heart's desire and then to want to be hurt. Someone's going to come along and take your job if you don't play. You answer that question for me." And he just looked at me and said, "Yeah, you're right."

I went back down to the minors. Kept getting cortisone shots regularly. It never got better. They loaned me to the Mets' AAA team. I went to Jacksonville and same old story. I just couldn't do it. Finally they had enough of me and the Angels wanted me to go to Boston's AAA club which was Toronto at the time. I said, "No, I've kind of made a fool of myself here. I'm coming home. My hand is hurtin' pretty bad and I can't do the job." So while I was en route driving back home from Florida to California they traded me to the Kansas City A's. They hadn't moved to Oakland yet. I called them and they wanted me to join their AAA team, which was Vancouver. So I joined Vancouver in Phoenix and they were not aware that I had a hurt hand. I was with them for about a month and of course they could see that my hand was in bad shape. They sent me to the Mayo Clinic and I saw two hand specialists and they both said it may heal, it may never heal. They said that the tendon was barely attached, too delicate to do surgery. They said, "We'll put it in a cast and see if immobilizing it will help." They did that and I came back home. After about six to eight weeks I went to see Kerlan and he took the cast off and then he had me go see a hand specialist. He said the same thing. "I wouldn't do surgery on that hand. You've got too many things there you could damage. You're just going to have to let it go and see what happens."

In the meantime, the A's sent me back to the Mayo Clinic to see the same two hand specialists and they said the same thing. It may heal, it may never heal, and sent me on my way. This was in '67, so I was ready to give it up. I thought, *Gosh, what am I going to do? I can't swing a bat.* The A's did send me a contract and a letter saying, "We know the diagnosis and prognosis of your hand, but we'd like you to come to spring training and let's see what happens."

So I did go to spring training with their AAA team and the hand did feel better. It was weak, but it was feeling better. It never did give me the trouble again that I had and it did heal, but it took some time. They sent me to their AA team in Birmingham and then, more than anything, it became a mental thing. I popped a muscle in my left shoulder and then I tore my left kneecap. So it was just a rough year, but the hand did heal.

In '69 I got drafted off the Birmingham A's by Houston's AAA team. I went to spring training, hand is fine. Season started and I got off to a rough start, wasn't hittin' too well. Manager put me on the bench. He could have used me as a DH, it was the first year for DH. Well, he finally did but in and out. I needed to get in every day and play. I had about a two-week period where we went on a road trip and I was hitting the ball very well, had nine homers. I had one bad game and he pulled me back out again. Shortly after that I tore my groin, not just pulled it, it tore real good. At the end of the year our manager told me, "I did you dirty." Now, he used another word but I'll use that one because he didn't play me.

In 1970 I tore the groin and went home. I went to my regular doctor and he thought I had a hernia. I had hernia surgery and I went back to spring training the next year. The groin's still botherin' me. I could run, but not well. It hurt. They wanted to put me on their AA team. It was embarrassing. I had to keep tellin' somebody that this was wrong, that's wrong, this hurts, that hurts. I was at the point where I could understand how these people in baseball must look at me. That bothered me a great deal. It was humiliating as well as very discouraging and finally I just said, "Look, I think it's best I just get my release. I can't keep going on like this." I was 26 at the time. Over the hill at 26. If I'd been more mature I probably would have stayed in there and maybe tried to hang around a little bit more. But all I was looking at was the way it was in the past, all the injuries, the frustration of it all. I thought I'm goin' the wrong way.

I got tired of it. I got tired of the whirlpools, cortisone shots, sittin' being taped up and this 'n' that. You know, all I dreamed about was playing major league baseball and havin' a successful career. Well, at this point it wasn't very successful.

I didn't know what to do. I did write some other ball clubs. I was kinda grabbin' at straws so to speak, just something. Maybe a change in organizations or something. Wishful thinkin'. You're hurt no matter where you go. I was hoping I could hang in there somehow. I didn't get any positive response. So I came home and had to go to work.

A friend of mine . . . he was a fellow that took Lou Gehrig's place, Babe Dahlgren. I was talkin' with him and he was tryin' to get indoor batting cages going, purchased a bowling alley. So I was helping him get that ready that summer. In the winter time I talked to Roland Hemond again and he got me to go down to Mexico, to play in the Mexican League. I went down there, I guess it was February or March of '71. Before I went down there I was helping Babe; I did all the painting on the inside and outside of the building. You know how you use those rollers? I got tennis elbow in my left elbow from pushing down on that thing. I went to see a local orthopedic surgeon that I had known for quite some time. He injected it with cortisone and I thought, well, that'll take care of it.

I went down to Mexico and this thing's still botherin' me. It's stiffin' up on me real bad. So believe it or not, I seen a doctor down there and he tried injectin' it. Well, it didn't work. He suggested they remove the bursa sac. So they did, down there. That was quite an experience. All these things were workin' on me mentally, made me frustrated, angry and I played a couple of games and I left. Left the ball club and came home.

I came home and I was going to this health club. I was talking to a guy there and I said, "Hey, I gotta go to work, I'm kind of lost, don't know what to do." He said, "Ever think about drivin' a truck?" I said, "Well, not really. My older brother did, but I've gotta do somethin'. I've gotta go to work, I've got responsibilities." There was a fellow there that he introduced me to that was a truck driver and he told me to go talk to his boss. They let me ride with a guy to learn how to drive. I've been drivin' a truck ever since.

Your truck route takes you by the Angels' ball park occasionally. How do you feel when you drive by?
    It hurts. It hurts.

JIM **RIVERA**

e was a 29-year-old rookie when he came up to the Browns in 1952. Jim would have made it sooner but he did four years in the army brig for attempted rape. He was traded to the White Sox that same year and was a mainstay of the "Go-Go" Sox of the fifties.

I was about four when my mother got hurt in New York City. They put her in the hospital and my dad put my sister Mary and I in an orphanage while she was recuperating. We thought we were only going to be there a little while, but wound up being there eleven years. When I came out in 1939 my mother had died and my dad remarried.

Did you learn to play baseball in the orphanage?
Yeah, but we didn't have any instructors. We had rocks for bases, a pick handle for a bat.

When I came to New York City, it was pretty hard to get a job. I started boxing. I went in the Golden Gloves. Went to the finals and got beat.

I was playing sandlot ball every Saturday and Sunday for a grocery store. They gave you all the milk and cookies and doughnuts you want. We didn't get no money. I went in the service the end of '42. When I came out in 1949 I got a chance to play ball for the Atlanta Crackers.

You got in some trouble while in the Army.
I was with some nurse. Nothing ever happened, but her being the captain's daughter, they pressed it and brought me to trial and

found me guilty of attempted [rape]. They couldn't prove it because she was still a virgin. I didn't hit her or nothing. No bodily harm. [I did] four and a half years. I was an army prisoner.

You came up in 1952 with the Browns. Your manager, Rogers Hornsby, said you were the only player worth paying to see but you were traded to the White Sox during the '52 season.

That was the "go-go" days for the White Sox. We were always behind the Yankees and Cleveland. They had such great ball clubs in those days. We had a great manager in Paul Richards, and then after that we had Al Lopez who I thought was a great manager. The guys played the game because they loved it. There's a lot of difference now. Then if you were batting real bad you weren't playing. You had your bags packed to go down. Now they've got these contracts that if they get an ingrown hair they don't want to play.

You went out there and did your job. Everybody was on time. Everybody was sober. There was no dope or anything going on like there is today. In those days they had bed check every night. Everybody minded his P's and Q's. Nobody fooled around.

The equipment and everything's changed today. I think the ball is livelier today. I've seen more guys hit home runs that couldn't have hit them in our time. The ball is juiced up. But that's what people want to see. I think that TV has really helped it a lot, but it's ruined it a lot.

It has helped because more people see it and like baseball. They come to the park. But then all that money; what happens when you get all that money and you can't handle it, you get in a lot of trouble. It's too much of a business now.

They've got so many darn fights all the time. They ought to have the managers or the owners have a meeting with each team and tell them to stop that. I got hit four or five times a year for Christ's sake. When the guy hit a home run in front of anybody the next guy expected to get knocked down. Ferris Fain used to get knocked down. They liked to hit him because he was a hothead. He'd try to hit the ball through the box and that wasn't his cup of tea.

My greatest [thrill] was in Cleveland when I hit that home run to cinch it against Mudcat Grant [to win the '59 pennant]. Ted Kluszewski got ahold of me—you know how big he was—in the shower. In those days I didn't drink and we had a fifth of Four Roses. He made us drink it, both of us, in the shower with our uniforms on. You're not going to argue with him, I'll tell you.

I'd like to be back there right now playing. Be a little younger and know a little bit more about baseball. These kids today have instructions in Little League and they get taught real good. We didn't have that when we were kids in New York City. We played stick ball. That's all. That time was not only beautiful, but everybody got along.

I'm proud of myself. I'm proud that one of the greatest owners of all time gave me a chance to play, Bill Veeck. I had some great managers with Richards, Al Lopez, Marty Marion and Hornsby. Then to play with all those nice guys. I can't remember [in the] ten years that I was there—maybe once—an argument in the clubhouse. Now that's unusual. Everybody come in and mind their own business. Got ready to play ball and when they were on the bench everybody was pulling for everybody.

I owe everything I've got to baseball. It's been great to me and I just wish that more kids would grow up and enjoy and love the game for what it is. Get everything they can out of baseball.

MARV **THRONEBERRY**

M arv was the first baseman for the original New York Mets in 1962. They finished the season at 40-120, and many consider them the most inept group to ever play major league baseball. Many believe Marv was the leader of the pack.

I don't think it was bad. I was still in the major leagues and they were a new club. I wasn't playing that much in Baltimore, so I was kind of looking forward to it.

A lot of it was blown out of proportion. We had a pretty good ball club. We didn't get a lot of breaks. Our pitchin' wasn't that great. I think we lost thirty-seven one-run ball games.

We had all the young writers and the Yankees had all the older writers. They were guys that had never followed a major league club before. Some of them was out of college looking to make a name for theirselves. Some of them was okay, but some of them, their ego I guess, they wanted to be big writers.

We'd lost so many ball games that I guess they got tired of writing so they would invent things that happened on the field. The next day we'd get to the ball park and say, "When'd we do that?" We had a lot of young kids that couldn't take it, so we took a lot off of them.

Casey played one ball game at a time. He was out to win just like we was. Everybody thinks that we didn't care whether we won or not, but [it was] like we were fighting for the pennant when you walk on the field. You don't want anybody to make you look bad. Just a lot of things happened that was blown out of proportion. When you take twenty-five ballplayers, and most of them had came up in different farm systems, each one is taught different things or different plays. So when you put them all together in six weeks of spring training you're gonna make mistakes.

Not too long ago I was looking in the paper and four clubs in the major leagues lost one hundred ball games. We only lost twenty more than that and these guys have been practicing for years. We scored a lot of runs. There was no problem with us scoring runs, it was just holding the runs.

I had problems with George Weiss [Mets GM]. Back then they paid what they wanted to. You didn't have an agent and they did you the way they wanted to. If you were asking for more money they could say, "Hell no"—you wasn't worth it. The last year I didn't have that bad a year. Nowadays, that would be worth a couple of million or more. Back then they treat you as just another cow in the pasture. They made all the money and you did all the work.

The fans were great. We had the National League fans. The Giants left New York, the Dodgers left New York. They wouldn't go to the Yankees because they were National League fans. So when we were formed they joined together. They [had] a National League club to call their own. They wanted us to win, but as long as they had their own club they didn't really get on you that much. New York people are funny anyway. They can get on you three times at bat and then you do something good and they're all for you. You learn to play with that.

UMPS

PAM **POSTEMA**

am umpired in the minors from 1977 through 1989. She worked AAA her last seven years and was finally released because the major leagues were not interested in her. She then filed a lawsuit alleging sexual discrimination.

For thirteen years she put up with more than her share of grief. She has no regrets but believes she should have been in the big leagues.

Pam is not optimistic about a female umpiring in the majors in the foreseeable future, convinced baseball wants to keep women in pink and out of blue.

I was thinking about going to college but I didn't know what I wanted to do. I saw this article in the Sunday paper about umpire school. I thought it was something that I would like. It was an outdoor job. It was baseball, which I loved.

They said they didn't have any women go to the school. So the more they said "No," the more I wanted to go. It took me a while, but finally Al Somers relented and let me into the school. I was good enough to get a job the next spring.

The school's only a six-week course. There were like 130 students that went my year. About 100 of us graduated. They rated and ranked you and then they filled the spots in the minor leagues with new umpires. I was lucky enough to get one of those slots in the Rookie League, in the Gulf Coast League.

I spent two years in the Gulf Coast League—A ball—then I moved up to the Florida State League—A ball—for two years and from there I went to the Texas League—AA—for two years and then I was in AAA in the Pacific Coast League for four years. The American Association for one, and then it merged with the International League, so the last two years I was in the American Association/International League. I did seven years in AAA.

Gary Darling was my partner in AA in the Texas League and he made the big leagues. Tim Welke was my first partner in the Rookie League and he made the big leagues. Gary Cederstrom was one of my partners and I worked with Billy Hohn and they made the big leagues.

It was a tough road the whole way. But I didn't care as long as I thought I was doing the job and my supervisors thought I was doing the job, but there were not too many umpire partners that were thrilled.

You have to work together on the field. Most of the time I was able to work with all my partners no matter how we thought about each other off the field. You have to be able to work on the field or you both look bad and you both go down. Except in the Pacific Coast League where Mark Johnson who made the majors refused to even acknowledge my presence in the locker room and talk to me. On the field we got in a big argument, started yelling at each other while the baseball game was going on.

But for the most part I was able to work with my partners. I didn't expect them to hold me up and I didn't expect to hold them up on the field. But you have to be able to work together on the field and I was always able to do that.

In minor league baseball the facilities aren't that great, let alone having separate locker rooms. So all the umpires were in one locker room. If there was no extra room for a shower we just had to step outside and take turns to dress and everything. It really wasn't any big deal. We'd get that question everywhere we went. "Do you guys take showers together?" That was the least of our problems—worrying about locker room facilities.

If you're having a good game the players stay off you. If you're having a bad game they're going to get on you. I think they probably tested me a lot more. The first close pitch I'd hear something more than if it was a male umpire. I sort of expected that and became a perfectionist from that. I wanted to get every pitch right.

You had a reputation for being better behind the plate than on the bases.

I got that tag early on in baseball. I did, by far, outshine on the plate. If they said anything they were going to say I was weak on the bases. I don't think later in my career that I was weak on the bases, but an average umpire on the bases.

I love to work the plate. You have to love to work the plate. I know a lot of umpires that didn't like to work the plate, just hated it. Working the bases to me was boring. You just have to be in the right position all the time to make the call. That's why they say anyone can umpire the bases, but to be a major league umpire that's where it's at, the plate. If you can work the plate you go to the big leagues.

I had a lot of confrontations. Pedro Gonzalez almost knocked me down with a bump early in my career in Rookie League. He was managing a team. That was the first time I'd ever been bumped, and was almost not a bump but an assault. He came at me full force and I thought, "Oh, he's going to stop any second now 'cause he's coming right at me and they can't touch an umpire." I'll tell you, a rookie umpire doesn't expect a guy coming at you full force. That was an awakening.

Bob Kluck in the Pacific Coast League was managing and he's kicking dirt all over my pants and spraying tobacco on me. I think he got suspended for that.

Larry Bowa kicking chalk on my pants and in the air and then it got in the eye of my partner. His tirades were tiresome.

Why were you released?

Because the National League and the American League were not interested in me. My league said if you've been in your AAA league for three years, and the big leagues are not interested in you, they will release you. But all they have to say is the American League or National League is still interested in that umpire, so they [then] stay longer.

I never regret anything I ever do. I loved my job. I loved umpiring or else I wouldn't have done it for thirteen years with low pay and abuse. But I don't regret it at all. I regret that I didn't make it to the big leagues. I hate to lose at anything. I feel I was qualified and good enough to umpire in the major leagues. I had a lot of good experiences. I got to umpire winter ball in Puerto Rico; in Colombia, South America; in Caracas, Venezuela. I would have never got to see any of those places and I've been all over the U.S. I really, really learned a lot from baseball.

I am disappointed with baseball. They don't want women in the game. I feel that if I couldn't make it, I don't see any other woman making it. I was as strong an umpire and person as anyone. It's weird when there are women firefighters and police officers; it's ludicrous that they don't want women umpires.

I came out of baseball with an anger and a desire to help the feminist cause. But I don't know what I want to do the rest of my life. I never knew when I was in baseball. I would never think about anything until tomorrow, so that's pretty much me. Put off anything you can until tomorrow.

DAVE **PALLONE**

A n umpire's life is tough enough; being a gay umpire is something else again. Dave Pallone is still gay, but no longer an umpire.

He was accused of being involved in a sex ring in upstate New York during the summer of 1988. Dave maintains his innocence, and according to him the league never presented him with any evidence to the contrary. Nonetheless, he was told his contract would not be renewed for the 1989 season. He threatened to sue; they offered a cash settlement and he took it.

During the ten years I was umpiring, I found other people that were gay in the front offices, playing and umpiring. Most of the time I found out either by seeing them in places that I traveled to or through mutual contact with people that we would associate with.

I am sure that other players that I knew confided with their friends, whether they be fellow teammates or peers, but it was more, "You don't bother me, I don't bother you." The same type of thing that is going on in the military. I didn't get involved with many players because it was always best that I didn't. Unfortunately, I didn't always keep to that rule.

I saw players later on in my career. I had an affair with one, well, actually there were two, but it wasn't an ongoing thing. I don't believe that it was wrong for umpires and players—they do it now—to associate with each other. Whether it be during the baseball season or after the baseball season. I think there's enough integrity in the game that it would never affect it. I felt that way the whole time I was there. I had no problem with it.

How would teammates handle a player that was gay?

I personally feel he wouldn't have a problem. His sexual orientation shouldn't make any difference, number one. Number two, his sexual orientation is not going to make him a better ballplayer or a worse ballplayer. If he gets his twenty wins, or he hits his thirty home runs or gets his hundred RBIs, I think the players are going to say, "We don't care as long as he's driving in these runs or getting these wins so we can win a pennant."

The fans are going to pick on anything. That's the way baseball fans have always been and that just gives them another thing to pick on. But if they didn't have that, they would find something else. And they are certainly not going to sit in their seats and put their hands on their rear ends and not applaud this man if he has a grand slam home run in the bottom of the ninth to win a game. They won't care about his sexual orientation.

I came up during the strike. I had a hard time with the other umpires. And then, forgetting my personal strife that I was going through inside, I had that problem. From 1983 through 1986, I was lucky enough to be partnered with Bob Engel and Paul Runge. They took me under their wing and accepted me for the type of job that I could do and gave me a chance to show the type of person I was. And they liked both. I looked forward to going to the ballpark every day, instead of hating it because I wasn't working with people I wanted to be with.

The rumors started right around the end of '86, early '87. I told Bob Engel late '87, I told Paul Runge early 1988. I told Bart Giamatti January 1988 that I was gay. It was before any of the controversies had come up.

It was time for me to tell some of the close people in my life so that they would stop wondering. I just felt so close to them that I . . . I wouldn't lose their friendship. But rumors started to come out and the Engels and the Runges and younger umpires whom I didn't have contact with read it in the papers or whatever, had no problem with it, because they don't have tunnel vision. And that's important.

John Kibler, Richie Garcia from the American League, Steve Palermo, American League, those type of guys [had problems with it]. Ed Vargo, who was my boss, despised me without question, he would not give me a break. He knew that with me working on John Kibler's crew in 1988 would make it very difficult, because John Kibler wanted nothing to do with me. The April 30th incident [his argument with Pete Rose], Kibler, who at that time was the crew chief, did not intercede with Pete and I getting in the shoving match, did not walk off the field with me—they did nothing to help me out in that situation. And yet, if I had not been a strikebreaker ten years earlier, they would have.

[It was a] close call at first. I delayed my call for about a second, two seconds, to make sure that I got the play right. It's not my responsibility to tell the first baseman that he should throw home if the run's going to score, that's his responsibility to know that I'm either calling the guy out or safe—which I called the guy safe—the eventual winning run scored and Pete and I got into a shoving match because he felt that I should have called the play earlier. Without question, I got the play right.

He pushed me, started to point in my face with his finger, so I started to point at him, he felt that I hit him and then he pushed me twice. He got suspended for thirty days and fined $10,000.

A little anecdote from that situation: Giamatti called me into the office later; they were going to fine me. Giamatti felt that I could have handled the situation a little bit better and he was going to fine me $100 and I said that was a joke. Either fine me or don't fine me. In essence, I fined myself $1,000 because I was telling him what he was doing was fining me a number that was just not real, especially if he felt that I was guilty. Fining Pete Rose $10,000 and fining me $100 just did not make sense. He would have gotten ridiculed not so much by the press, because maybe the press would not have known, but other owners, other people that he would have to tell. We made enough money to pay a $1,000 fine if we were wrong.

The heat came in mid-September when major league baseball asked me to take a leave of absence the last two weeks of the season. But in the interim, from around the All-Star break until that time, they were investigating a rumor that I had been involved in a teenage sex ring, which I was not, and I proved that beyond a shadow of a doubt. However, I was called into the office and they told me that I was under investigation for something in upstate New York, but they never told me what it was. I kept asking them, "How can you continually tell me that you don't know, but yet you're telling me that I am under investigation? How come no one has called me? If the State Police in New York are investigating me for something, or someone is investigating me, why hasn't anyone contacted me? Why is just major league baseball contacting me?" I repeatedly asked the head of security for the major leagues—actually for the commissioner's office—repeatedly asked Giamatti, asked everybody, "Have you heard anything, do you know anything, is anything going on?" And they kept telling me, "No."

Mid-August I didn't know anything. All of a sudden I get hit with this bombshell in September. I found out through my own investigators that major league baseball knew all of July and all of August what was happening, but they just did not tell me. It's my contention, if you look at the proof, that they were trying to hold up everything so it would blow up, so that way they would have a reason to dismiss me. It's interesting that everybody thinks that I resigned, while the papers show that I retired, but I was forced to retire. They were not going to renew my contract and I was going to take them to court.

I was completely cleared of any wrongdoing. I wasn't even investigated. The District Attorney of New York publicly stated that I had never been under investigation for any wrongdoing, period. But major league baseball said that they had evidence that I was involved with something and I could not understand how they could possibly have evidence about something.

I went to major league baseball and said, "Bring the people that are spreading these rumors around, bring them to me, tell me who they are, have them come face-to-face with me." But they never did.

Bart Giamatti and I had a tremendous rapport. I really felt very close to him. Most people that have read my autobiography feel that I was too nice to him, but he was always wonderful to me. I believe it was the owners that pulled the trigger to the gun that he was holding.

As long as I was in baseball, almost twenty years, I came to one conclusion: it will not give you anything for nothing. If they felt that I was wrong, that I had done something wrong, if they had evidence like they say they had on Pete Rose, they would have thrown away the key on me. They would never give me a dime. Never. Not in a million years. No way. They gave me a sum of money that isn't enough for me to live [on]. At that time it sounded great, it was enough for me to walk away and try to start a whole new life. But I haven't been able to do that, because my heart still is at Wrigley Field. I would be back in the game yesterday if I could.

I am still trying to find an attorney that will look at all the papers that I signed and look me straight in the eye and say, "Fuck what you signed—you know your rights were abrogated, you never lose your civil rights as a human being in America, let's go get them."

There isn't anyone out there that wants to not so much take on major league baseball, but do it maybe for nothing. Because if I lose I would never be able to pay him, and a lot of attorneys want money up front; they want $30,000-$40,000-$50,000 up front. I just don't have that kind of money.

Believe it or not, I have some wonderful gratification out of not being in baseball because of my second calling, I guess you can say. I travel to universities all over the country and I speak to students about human rights, about how to feel good about themselves—about their sexual orientation. I talk about the prevention of teenage suicide.

Since the writing of my autobiography I have received over 40,000 letters from people of all ages looking for help and wanting to talk to someone. That, plus writing another book, keeps me busy, keeps me financially secure to the point where I'm not worrying where my next dollar is. The problem I have is I would like to be in something that I worked very hard for and want to be in; major league baseball is my passion.

JOHN **KIBLER**

H e was a National League umpire from 1965 to 1989. He worked four World Series and four All-Star Games. John was one of the best.

It is not an easy life. You are away from home more than seven months a year, the pay is just all right and everyone is on your back. To make matters worse at the end of the season your performance is critiqued by the managers and coaches and sent to the league office.

I grew up in upstate New York and we didn't get much chance to play baseball because of the winters. I went to all the tryout camps in those days. Everybody used to tell me to go home and practice some more and then come back. I'd go back, and finally I had to go into the service.

In the service I played ball with a lot of big league and AAA ballplayers. They told me, "You're not good enough to be a ballplayer, but as much as you love baseball you should go into umpiring. Go to umpire school." I never realized there was such a thing as umpire schools.

When I came out of the service, I went back to the New York State Police. While we were in the academy I ran into a guy by the name of Al Salerno. Al was from Utica, New York and I had played baseball against him in the semi-pro leagues. On his desk was a brochure from Al Somers Umpire School. He and I got talking and I told him I was interested. After we'd put in a little over a year and a half in the State Police we both decided to quit and go to umpire school. Al went the year before I did. We were both fortunate to become major league umpires.

I had seven years in the minor leagues. I was in the Georgia-Florida League first. Then the Pioneer League. I went to the Sally League and worked two years there. In '62 I went to the American Association. In '63 I went to spring training with the National League [with] Billy Williams, Doug Harvey and Doug got the job. I went to the International League and came up and worked about a week at the end of that season. The following spring I was going to go to the big leagues and replace Jocko Conlon, but Jocko asked to work another year so I ended up back in the International League and came up at the end of the year for about a month. Then in 1965 I became a regular member of the staff.

They send out a grading form once a year to the general managers, managers and coaches. Isn't that a great grading? I told [Chub] Feeney when he was there, "All you're running is a popularity contest. When I get my ratings next year and somebody's team rates me bad, I want you to tell me who they are so that next year I can be nice to 'em so I can get a higher rating." He didn't like that too much. We're the only sport not graded by our peers.

I guarantee you, you could go to half of the ballplayers and say, "What do you think about John Kibler's umpiring?" They'd say, "Who is he?" Unless you're a "Dutch" Rennert who has that great voice and all that action on the field, nobody knows who you are. Here's a guy that's going to vote on you and he doesn't know anymore about umpiring than the clock on my wall.

In an average game, working behind the plate, how many balls and strikes are you going to miss?

A lot of times we'd say, "Oh, six a side. Boy, great game." It's all according to the pitching you get. Some games you're going to miss four a side, five a side. Other games you're going to maybe miss two or three. If the pitching's good, guys swing at the ball so you don't have that many decisions; plus the ball's always around the plate.

You're getting 3-2 on every batter. Everybody's complaining about the time of games—that's what makes the time of games go up. It's not the umpires. Of course, the players don't help anymore. They don't want to get in [the batter's box]. You don't have pitchers who'll throw the ball over the plate continuously.

They're always saying the umpires have gotta speed up the game. There's no way in the world an umpire can speed up the game. You try to get the guy in the batter's box, you try to break up a meeting on the mound . . . then you're invariably in an argument. Then you're going to throw somebody out. Now you've delayed the game longer. The meetings on the mound, all the running back and forth every pitch. The catcher going out. Guys not coming out of the dugout 'til the pitcher is done and not being ready to get in the box and staying in the box. Those are the things they have to address to speed up the game.

Durocher was always the most unfair person on the field. Off the field you couldn't want a nicer guy. He'd say we deserved more money. But once you put a uniform on him, he was tough. And very unfair.

I've heard it from [Al] Barlick and all those guys that umpired years with him. He had only one thing in mind . . . he was going to win. No matter what it cost him.

I had an argument with Ron Santo in Chicago one day. Ron said he tagged the guy and I said, "No, you didn't." He and I went back and forth. I didn't run Santo because he never swore. I said, "Ron, you missed the guy . . . " we're going on. Now Durocher's standing there. The next day Durocher puts in the paper, "Umpire John Kibler certainly missed the play and Ron Santo called him every name in the book and he wouldn't run him."

That's a tough thing to put up with as an umpire. If you're wrong and the guy tells you you're wrong and you know you're wrong, well fine, but when you're not wrong and things go on like that. In those days what recourse did we have, we just kept our mouths shut.

Walter Alston was great. Gene Mauch was an outstanding manager. Probably the most astute with the rules, but couldn't win those games when he had to. He was tough. He could give you a real tough day.

The best baseball athlete I saw was Clemente. Mays was outstanding, but he was on the way down when I came in, where Clemente was just coming into his own. Between he and Rose, it's tough to make a choice. But Clemente had great skills.

You know, ninety-five percent don't know the rules. I've had people in the big leagues fifteen years asking me . . . like one guy asked me if he bunts is it an infield fly? This guy was a catcher. It's just amazing—they have no idea of the rules.

Manny Sanguillen swung at anything that came near the plate. He was a great hitter. It's not that he didn't know the strike zone. He just wanted to hit and he didn't care if the ball was down the middle or not.

I've often said I wished hitters would just go back and look at the Pittsburgh Pirate clubs from those years. Even though they weren't winning, they had .300 batting averages, five or six guys on the team. They weren't waiting for one special pitch and get 3 and 2 and get called out on a close pitch and moan and scream. I think that aspect of the game has really gone. Everybody [now] thinks it's gotta be one pitch, where those guys just got up and when a pitch was in the area they swung at it.

Tim Foli was one of the toughest guys to deal with in my career. You couldn't please Tim if you called a pitch eight feet outside a ball. Any time there was an argument he was right in the middle of it . . . just really tough to control.

Once in Pittsburgh we had a play at the plate and he was playing shortstop and I was working third. He came over and said, "Would you explain the rule to me?" I said, "I'm going to explain the rule to you and tell you what happened in this situation but you're not to go anyplace but back to your position." He said, "Okay." So I explained it to him. I no more than got done and he took off and tore for home plate. Started hollerin' and screamin'. I'd just told him the guy got the play right. When he came back out towards shortstop, I walked over to him and said, "Don't ever speak to me again as long as you're in this game."

We went three years before he finally said to me, "John, can I talk to you?" I said, "I don't think so." The next day I said, "What would you like to say?" He said, "I want to apologize." I said, "It's too late." And he said, "Well, I just don't feel right." I said, "All right. As far as I'm concerned, it's forgotten. I'll speak to you. I'll say hello. But that's all." I spoke to him the rest of my career, but . . .

Some catchers don't even talk to you. Steve Yeager was probably the greatest. He was always talking to you about something. Talking to the batters, talking to everybody. He loved to talk. Some of them would say, "Would you shut up, Yeager." For a good catcher, and a good guy, he talked as much as anybody.

Andy Messersmith. I had him the last game of the year. He was gettin' beat 4-1 or something and going for his twentieth win. I called a pitch a ball and he started off the mound and I said, "Whoa, whoa. Hold up right there. Don't come any further or I'm going to run you." I said, "The ball was outside," whatever. He says, "I'm coming further." I said, "Now, don't. Because I don't want to have to run you out of this game." He came almost to the plate and I just held my hand up, didn't say anymore. When he got to home plate he said, "That ball...." I said, "You're done."

Here's a guy going for his twentieth game. If he takes a step off the mound and says something you're going to holler at him to get back on the mound. But when he starts coming in toward home plate he's automatically gone.

He went goofy. Walter came out and said, "John, this guy is going for his twentieth win." I said, "No, Walter, he was."

You know what happened? The Dodgers scored six runs in the eighth inning and won the game. I doubt if he'd have been around then, but Walter might have left him in knowing he's going for his twentieth.

Not a bad guy when he pitched, but the worst on the bench was Bob Gibson. He was forever saying things from the bench to you and hollerin' at the other club. When he was on the mound he'd look at you now and then and be mad, but just get back and throw again. But he was always screamin' from the bench.

I have to say Koufax was the best pitcher. There were so many good guys around then. You had Koufax, Drysdale, Marichal,

Gibson. I came up when Spahn was still around, who was great. There were just so many good pitchers in those days.

I was a young umpire just coming in and I worked Drysdale and Koufax a hundred times probably in spring training. I was at Dodger spring training down in Vero Beach. They would leave Koufax behind when the club went on the road because they wanted him to pitch 'cause he couldn't throw the ball inside your house and as young umpires we really took a beating because he was wild.

They wanted him to get more pitching. We would have to umpire the game and he used to beat us to death. The poor catchers and us because that curve ball would break about fifty feet and nobody could catch it. The fast ball would be moving and nobody could catch it. So when he finally got control of his game, it was amazing. I remember working a game in Chicago where he threw a couple of curve balls that bounced out in front of the plate. I said, "John [Roseboro, Dodger catcher], I remember when he used to do that." And he says, "Yeah, it looks like he's not going to have too good a day today. We better go to the fast ball." He pitched a two-hitter, and I don't think he threw three curve balls the rest of the day.

Philadelphia was tough. Philadelphia they say is the greatest doubleheader town in the world. Everybody wanted that two-for-one deal. They all came out to watch two games for the price of one. They love their baseball there. Everybody says they were the hardest and I would say that's true. They are the most astute fans. They knew their baseball in that town.

Everybody used to ask what's your favorite city and I used to say Chicago. They'd say, "Why Chicago?" 'Cause they have all day games. It's great to go in there and live like a human being. You could go out and eat and then go to work and come home like everybody else. Instead of hanging around all day and then go to work.

In the minor leagues you go away and come back four months later. You certainly couldn't get home. You didn't have any money. I was pretty fortunate. After I got married my first year in baseball I took my wife with me every year. I put her in a town.

I got to see her only when I was in that town, but at least she was with me. Most guys went away for those four months and never got back home.

I'm not happy with the game the way it is today. I think the money has put so much pressure on the players that they've taken all the fun out of the game. Everybody has incentives in their contracts so they want to get at bat this many times, they want to get this many hits or this many walks or this many strikeouts or this many whatever. They can't do it and they're trying to look for somebody to blame. I don't blame the players for taking the money. If somebody would offer me that tomorrow I'd jump at it. I'm certainly not going to say, "Well, no, I'm not worth that much." But the fun has gone out of the game. When there's a borderline pitch, it's not like he'd turn around and say, "Where's that pitch, John." And I'd say, "Hey, tough pitch." "Yeah, well, that's the way it is. Tough pitches come, you know." You'd talk back and forth.

Now it's, "Where the hell was that pitch?" Now you've got the umpire on the defensive and he's going back at ya, and the first thing you know you've got a big argument. So all that's gone out of the game. All the problems that baseball's having and doesn't address. It's just a whole different game to when I started.

THE MEDIA

ROGER **KAHN**

I believe the finest baseball book ever written is *The Boys of Summer* by Roger Kahn, published in 1971. Many agree. The book is about his coming to terms with his father's death and revolves around this and the father/son relationship, not only his, but of many of the Brooklyn Dodger players he visited.

But it is more. It represents simpler times, when there was a certain civility in America that is now missing. When the World Series was played outside, during the day, on the grass. When people knew players' batting averages and not their salaries. People owned teams, not corporations. The sky was bluer and the grass was greener.

> *I see the boys of summer in their ruin*
> *Lay the gold tithings barren,*
> *Setting no store by harvest; freeze the soils.*
>
> **DYLAN THOMAS**

Sport magazine asked me to do a story for their twentieth anniversary. I said, "If you pay my way to go out and see Billy Cox, who I always admired, I'll do it." The editor said, "Yes, sure, we'll pay your way." I went out and saw Cox and was a little taken aback by the fact that he's a substitute bartender. He looked very different than the third baseman I remembered because he had grown a belly like Falstaff. There were a couple of old, retired railroad characters sitting at the bar wearing the striped caps that railroad men wore. They looked at me as though I were a communist spy. This is in the American Legion Club in Newport, Pennsylvania. When I walked in, Billy Cox with Falstaff's belly ran out from behind the bar and said, excited to see me as I was to see him, "You've seen me...could I play ball?" gesturing toward the railroad guys. I said in shock, "Billy, you were the best damn glove I ever saw." He turned to the railroad men and said, "You hear that? A New York writer said that."

That was kind of an epiphany. I thought, *God, it has no reality unless I'm here to confirm it, and usually I'm not here.* So that sat in the back of my head, and that is sort of the prologue to how the whole idea began.

I had a fairly comfortable sixties thanks to the *Saturday Evening Post's* great editor, Otto Frederich. I was an editor-at-large and covered the Eugene McCarthy campaign. I covered the Barry Goldwater campaign. I was a very successful magazine writer, doing sports only from time to time; mostly doing general pieces.

Now it came time for the *Saturday Evening Post* to die. I'm looking around at three children, an ex-wife, a monthly alimony bill, and a then present-wife who was disinclined to work. I figured, well, I guess this is going to be a life spent at *Time* magazine writing drab pieces about foreign policy and being rewritten. That's what you're going to do and you're going to get these kids through college. Then I thought, "But before I do, a word or two before I go . . ." I think that's from *Othello*. There was once a team and there were these people and their lives were of some significance. Before I fall into the drab, alcoholic world of news magazine writing to support all of these people, I want to set these guys down. That was the beginning. I wrote a one-and-a-half page letter beginning with the Dylan Thomas poem. I think the advance was $25,000. Spectacularly small when you realize I had to go all across the United States to see the people.

That was germinal. I said, "This will be the last time I'll ever write a book. This is the book I want to write. It struck me that growing up with a father who had been a college ballplayer, baseball was a metaphor for many things in the prime of father and son. I then began to add growing up in Brooklyn. But the idea was this is the last book I'll do before I get roped into group journalism.

Carl Erskine told me he talked to you while you were writing The Boys of Summer *and you told him you had gone dry. You were having trouble finishing the book.*

I'm glad he remembers that. I was marching along from page 450 to 451 and people may think that it's easier to go from 450 to 451 than it is to go from 1 to 2, particularly people who have never written a book. It isn't really easier. The book was getting longer and I wasn't getting nearer the end. I was writing more and more pages and the end was nowhere in sight, and some of the stories were sort of troubling to set down: Clem Labine's son losing a leg, my visit with Campanella.

I went for no real reason to a Sports Lodge B'nai B'rith dinner honoring Gil Hodges. I just did it to get out of the house and there was Erskine. Carl and I were friends and he said, "How's it going?" and I said, "It's getting longer but I'm not getting nearer the end." We went to Toots Shor's restaurant and sat. We had a couple of drinks, so I can't recall exactly what Erskine said, but he gave a pep talk that would have been worthy of Knute Rockne. He said, "Of course it's hard. But we all talk and we all know what you're doing and the whole team is counting on you so that we will not be forgotten. So that our grandchildren will know that we were here. Everybody's counting on you. Now come on." He did that in a kind of gentle but insistent way. "Come on now, we don't want this to vanish from history. These were wonderful times. Important times in a whole bunch of ways, and you're the only person who can do it. We're all counting on you." That was the thrust of his speech and the next morning when I wiped the cobwebs out of my face I sat down and I finished the book in the next few months.

An early idea was that when the cheering stops, their lives don't end. How do they go on with the rest of their lives?

Duke Snider was unhappy with the way he appeared in the book. He was going through the bankruptcy of a bowling alley and it was not a glorious time in his life, and he would have wanted to be recorded at a more glorious moment, such as today, or when he went to a ball game with George Bush. He said, "You know, I really should have emphasized that even though the bowling alley went bankrupt, I paid all of the local people before I took the bankruptcy so that the only people who were stuck in the bankruptcy were large corporations that could afford it."

I'd heard Duke complain on and off for a lot of years. I said, "Let me tell you something, Duke, the book is not about you." He said, "What's it about?" I said, "It's about me coming to terms with my father's death." He said, "Well, I suppose you can read it that way, too." That is what it's about. And all the rest is around that.

Otto Friedreich, who was a wonderful editor, said was I aware of the father and son theme through the book? Labine and his kid, Jackie Robinson and his kid, Erskine and his kid. Of course I was. I'm not totally unconscious.

It's about me and my dad and other kids and other dads. But what an author sets out to do, that's only one vote. What it means to other people is what it means to them. So there's a universal quality that keeps going and people find different things in it. What it is to me was twenty years after Gordon Kahn died, sitting down and coming to terms with that.

That must have been wonderful for you to be working at a young age for the Herald Tribune *and be covering the Dodgers. They were your father's team. To have been covering the Dodgers must have been like a ballplayer playing in the big leagues while his father was still alive. That must have been a nice feeling.*

It really was. Of course, I had this remarkable opportunity and I probably didn't want to face it at the time, but I also had an opportunity to fall on my face every morning in full view of 500,000 readers. So there was a certain healthy terror in the experience also. But yes, I remember this age-old balance between father and son. Some people write about it as when the son begins to defeat the father on a tennis court. I was getting him baseball tickets instead of him getting me baseball tickets. I was seven years old when he took me to the games. Now I was saying, "You want to go to a game, Dad, I'll get you behind first base, or behind the plate if you want to watch the pitching." It was very pleasant. At the same time he was a little bit put off by it. "Who is this kid to get me tickets. I saw the Dodgers in Washington Park before Ebbets Field was built. Who is this cheeky young man to do these things. It's my son, but I can get my own tickets." It was spikey in a good way. It was passing to the next generation. Suddenly the next generation could get the good seats for the ball games.

You visited with many of the old Dodgers in writing the book. What were some of the more poignant visits?

I'll never forget Labine weeping. Sitting in this country club. Labine is a successful and gifted man. A man of some dignity and well-dressed, poised, charming . . . he began to tell me about his son. How his son lost his leg. As he was telling me this story he began to weep. It's something to cry about. Your son losing his leg in Vietnam. I had that feeling of looking at somebody in a family in terrible, terrible pain and seeing how that wicked Vietnam War had come to Woonsocket, Rhode Island. It didn't only come to San Francisco and Chicago and Washington where the big parades and big protests were. Here this war, which should never have been fought, had come and taken the leg of a kid and opened all kinds of grief. That was terribly poignant.

I remember having a catch with Shuba. But the thing was going downstairs and the string suspended from the ceiling with a knot and I was swinging the bat and George is giving this tip about top hand over early and we're sweating. We're not kids, and he's saying, "That's it. Now you got it. Now you got it." And I say, "God, George, if I'd only known this twenty years ago." He said, "Come on, the fast ball's by the two of us." That was poignant.

[Joe] Black talking at length about prejudice in less dramatic terms than Robinson, but how he had found out about American racism. That was very lasting.

I'll never forget leaning against the Pine Oak in the Ozarks with Preacher Roe talking about the way it was in the Ozarks. Just listening to his stories, and then he looks around the ballfield and says, "It's all overgrown." And I said, "Is that rye grass?" which is kind of provincial eastern. And he said, "No, no, that's sage. You leave a field alone, the sage will take over." I said, "No ball games here now." He said, "No, they all go over to Memphis for the rock music. Same thing here as at Ebbets Field, there'll never be a ball game played here again." You know, "Ulp." There were a lot of "ulps."

Furillo was putting elevator doors in the World Trade Center. Obviously, doing a good job because the elevator doors did not collapse.

His place on earth was right field in Ebbets Field where he was the Emperor. He was a very complex sort of fellow in that he was a political conservative. Originally was a little put off by blacks coming into the game. When he found out that blacks were people, he warmed up every day with Campanella. He was enough of a man to get over the prejudices of his childhood. He'd only gone to the eighth grade. He didn't play bridge; some of the other Dodgers did and he felt he was an outsider.

He got hurt. The Dodgers released him. He read the contract, and you can't be cut the year you're hurt. You gotta be paid for the year. He went to a lawyer and there was litigation against the Dodgers. There's conflicting stories from Furillo and Bavasi, but anyway, the effect of the litigation was really to have Furillo labeled at the very least a troublemaker. When the Dodgers released him, he won something from the suit and he also won an unconditional release, and he wrote longhand letters to every other team. Nobody answered him. Not politic, you know. If you get very mad at a publisher, let your agent shout. Don't you do it.

So, Carl, doing what he thought was right and probably was right, got himself more or less blackballed. There was this period of, "I'm not going to play in their goddamn old timers' games," and a period of great anger. Toward the end he mellowed a bit. I saw him a couple of years before he died. He was working as a night watchman. Had a little money, not much. He worked four nights a week and he had chronic leukemia. Not the kind of leukemia that kills you in a year and a half. The kind you have for twenty years—and he died of a heart attack.

He was a tremendous American primitive.

I've re-thought O'Malley for *The Era*. I like him much more. I've gotten some new stuff which I didn't have at the time of *The Boys of Summer* relating to his dealings with Robert Moses. But O'Malley was an entrepreneur. A robber baron, I guess. I have a picture of him [in *The Boys of Summer*] underneath a sable antelope which he shot in Africa. That's not an accident.

I thought that was a metaphor for Brooklyn.

That's it. That's what I meant. That's what I had in mind. There were some things I don't really understand about him. His wife had cancer of the voice box or the larynx and it was removed. So she could not speak above a very quiet whisper and you had to be around Kay O'Malley for quite awhile before you could understand what she was saying. She had, nonetheless, built a life for herself on Long Island where she was in a garden club and did the kind of garden club things. A very nice lady. And she built a circle of friends. I am told that when he said he was going to California she wept and wept.

When O'Malley moved to California he lived in a hotel for a couple of years, and God, any night I spend in a hotel is a night misspent. He was living in the Statler-Hilton.

So a great adventurer and devoid of sentiment. Just devoid of it. But I've heard of some good things that he has done relating to individuals.

If you could do it again, what should have happened was the Dodgers stayed in Brooklyn. Dodgers should have stayed in Brooklyn and the Mets should have been in Los Angeles. Let the people in Los Angeles have the last place Mets for three years.

I mean, that would be logical. Ford Frick chose not to block this. I think he could have blocked it. I think the current climate of the courts is to limit the power of a commissioner, but I think that was a different time and if Frick had said this is not in the best interest of baseball for you to move, Walter, that would have been the end of that. Walter would not have been able to move.

If I had stayed on the paper and continued to travel with the team I would probably have been as angry as people like Dick Young and others at the departure of the team because they were faced with the dreadful fate of covering amateur golf. But I had tired of traveling with the team. To this day, I love a ball game, but not six days a week. So, I had gone over to *Newsweek* and I was doing a lot of other things. I had moved out of Brooklyn and it didn't hit me viscerally that the Dodgers left. I guess I was sad. Only in later years did I begin to say, "Goddamn, this is really an awful thing that somebody comes in and says 'I'm a fan' and wraps himself in Brooklyn patriotism and then marches off to California in search of gold."

This book changed my life in a lot of ways and it'll get me a little bit of financial comfort. I'm more proud really that I was able to do what I wanted to do and become a writer. That I was able to realize a dream that began when I read the poetry of John Keats and said, "Well, that's what I'm going to do." It didn't turn out that I was going to write "Ode to a Nightingale," but I've written numbers of good things.

Red Smith was wonderful to me. John Lardner was wonderful to me. I think of John Lardner often. You don't become a writer by accident and get that good. You've got to want to do it and work at it and work the craft. John worked it and of course died very young. I'm proud to be in the same racket as Robert Frost, John Lardner, William Shakespeare—that's what I'm proudest of. That I've lived all my life as a writer, never really wanted to be anything else. Maybe play third base a little bit.

PHIL ALDEN **ROBINSON**

A female student was once asked by Howard Koch, one of the writers of *Casablanca,* why she kept going back to see the film. She replied, *"Casablanca* has all those graspable values which we can no longer find today."

Although *Field of Dreams* was made nearly fifty years later, it too fits this very apt description. Loyalty, devotion, passion, commitment and belief in a dream are as important today as in 1942—but now harder to find.

Phil Alden Robinson, as writer and director, does a masterful job of weaving these values throughout *Field of Dreams.* The result is one of the most poignant films ever made. The movie points out that America is forever changing, but that baseball serves as a constant. People continue to relate to the game because it is not altered.

For anyone who played (or didn't play) catch with their father, the movie's last line rivets the soul. It is one of the simplest lines ever delivered, but also one of the most complex and heartwarming— the common denominator for so many that saw the film: "Dad, do you want to have a catch?"

Someone had given me the book, I think back in 1982, and said "You really ought to read this—it's a great book." I said, "What's it about?" She said, "It's about this farmer." I said, "Nah . . . I'm not really interested in farmers." And she said, "No, wait, he hears a voice." "Gee, I really don't think this is for me." She insisted that I read the book. I took it home that night, grumblingly opened it up and it was the first time in my life I literally could not put a book down. It was the most original and moving thing I'd ever read.

131

I tried to get people interested in setting it up as a feature and nobody in town was interested. I spent a couple of years trying to get people interested. Finally, 20th Century Fox bought it. Hired me to write it. That was about '85 or '86. Then I sat down and wrote the screenplay and 20th put it in what's called "turnaround," meaning they weren't going to make it. So the producer I was working for took it to Universal, who loved the script and said let's make the film. That was, I think, the end of '87.

You were the writer and director. The novel was Shoeless Joe *by W. P. Kinsella. Is the film much different from the book?*
It's pretty similar. Only two big changes, but they both are in keeping with the spirit of the book. In the book the appearance of Ray's father is not a surprise to Ray or to the reader. Ray, in fact, asks Shoeless Joe in the first chapter, "Would you let my father come play with you?" And the father shows up maybe two-thirds of the way through the book. Kinsella, being a writer, was more interested in the plight of J. D. Salinger who is the character in the book that we fictionalized as Terrance Mann in the movie. The book ends with J. D. Salinger being invited by the players to walk off into the corn with them and he goes with them.

When I sat down to make a movie out of this, the main thing was to deliver what the book delivers, but build up the father-son issue. There are some other characters in the book that are not in the movie. I think it's pretty much in keeping with the spirit —in large extent the letter of the book. A lot of the dialogue from the book is in the movie.

The ballfield we built is actually on two farmers' farms. The farmhouse we used for the movie is owned by the man who owns the infield and right field. But left field and center field belong to the farmer next door. After we finished shooting, which was late summer of '88, the farmer next door decided he wanted to plant corn there again. The first summer after the movie came out, that would be the summer of '89, there was only half a field. A lot of tourists came and greatly surprised the farmer next door who decided the following year that he would set aside that land and let the full ballfield exist.

One of the great things about this story is that it is open to a lot of interpretation. Some really do miss the mark . . . I should-n't say miss the mark. They were certainly not intended by me. I've read some fundamentalist religious interpretations, believe me, I didn't intend. But the more secular ones are on the nose.

I was trying not to think too much about the message 'cause I have the example of the book before me . . . of people being able to read into it what they would. One of the things that I loved about the magic in the book—no attempt is ever made to explain it. We never tried to say, "Who is this?" "Where does this voice come from?" "Why has it happened?" "How does he go back in time?" All that is left unexplained, and therefore subject to inter-pretation, and I like that. I think it's a valid way to tell a story. Also, I think had we tried to explain it we would have failed. You can't explain that stuff.

I think a lot has to do with the role that simply having a catch plays in the life of a father and a son. It's part of the process of growing up—playing catch with your father. Just the memory of it harkens you back to what seemed to be simpler times; they might in fact have been simpler. I think there's something in us that would love to believe they were and somehow recapture, if not the reality, then at least the impression of that.

One of the best reactions I ever had was from a woman friend of mine who said, "You know, I never obviously played catch with my dad. But when I saw that scene I started to think about all the hours I spent in the kitchen with my mother learning how to cook. I started to cry at that." And I thought, she's got it.

Shoeless Joe Jackson and Ray's father both ask if the ballfield is heaven. Ray both times said, "No, it's Iowa." Were you saying that heaven, or contentment, is anyplace where you're happy and where your dreams come true?

Sure. Sure. It's interesting the way those two scenes work, the first time Shoeless Joe says, "Is this heaven?" and Kevin says, "No, it's Iowa," it gets a good laugh. A good, honest, warm laugh. It's like a joke. It's like Kevin's character saying, in essence, this is not-heaven. This is like this mundane, boring place. At the end of the film, when his father says, "Is this heaven?" and he says, "No, it's Iowa," it's more like making the connection between heaven and Iowa, saying, "Yeah, it may seem like heaven, but in fact it's Iowa and that's good enough for me."

When we were shooting I was dissatisfied and I didn't think it was going to be very good. I was pretty depressed the whole time we were shooting. I thought I wasn't getting it. When we finished the film I thought it was okay. I really didn't think it was going to have much of an impact. When we started to screen it for people and they started to react the way they did, it's the most wonderful feeling. I'm not talking about people in the business, but the letters that we would get from people around the country and around the world, many of which were very similar. A lot of letters from guys saying, "I just wanted to tell you I haven't talked to my father in many years and after I saw the film I called him up and said, let's have a catch." I thought that's the best thing that could happen. I'll take that over the Academy Award any day.

It's so fulfilling and such a wonderful feeling to think that you had a little part in actually changing something. It's Kinsella's story. He gets the lion's share of the credit. But what a thrill to be part of that.

One review I read was very smart and said this film was about legacies. It's about a father's legacy to a son. It's about the legacy of baseball. It's about the legacy of the sixties and how to stay true to some of those ideals and somehow all those things dovetail. I think a lot of it is just about being true to yourself. The idea of not giving up your dreams.

MIKE **ROYKO**

he late **Mike Royko was a lifelong baseball fan, but one of his problems was the lack of loyalty among today's players.**

I wouldn't want to be a baseball manager. I was a softball manager and my system was very simple: If a guy dogged it, I threw him off the team. You can't do that in baseball because the guy's got a contract guaranteed this year, next year, the year after. Baseball managers are very limited. That's why they keep switching them around and changing 'em. Look at the Yankees. The Cubs have run through so many managers. If I were a baseball manager, I would just make out the lineup, hope they played well, and save as much of my paycheck as I could.

If I were a general manager I would hire somebody like Frank Howard to be my manager. I would hire the biggest, meanest, toughest guy I could find. Even if he wasn't bright I could always get some coaches who were bright to help him think. But I'd hire a guy maybe 6'8", 320 pounds, with a vicious temper, and if a guy screwed up, did something really dumb on the field, as he was walking back to the dugout, this big manager would come out and punch him right in the face, knock him down. The fans would love it, the fans would cheer. They'd love the manager. If he's big enough and mean enough, just beat up the players. Yeah, that's what I'd do, I would just hire a huge thug as my manager. I'd make it a Mafia guy. Have him pack a gun and say real quietly, "You do that again and I'll kill you."

I think death threats would be the best solution. I think that's what I'd do. If I were a manager I would get guys who were collectors for the Mafia, loan shark collectors, and I'd hire them as my coaches. A guy screwed up they'd go over and say to him, "You did it again, and that's our last warning, the next time I shoot you in the kneecap." It might work. I don't know, what else could work with modern ballplayers?

I think death threats would do it. The guy goes up to pinch-hit and strikes out. Three pitches. Then he goes home and finds his garage is burned down. You know, a little arson. Maybe, a phone call: "When you went in there today, you shook off the catcher and then you threw a gopher ball. We know where your children go to school."

Many players have not learned [that] if a pitcher throws four bad pitches you get to walk to first base. I might bring in a mathematics instructor. Four balls, it's just like a single, you walk down, you don't have to run [to first].

I would ban all rings where they put them through their ears or noses; no gold chains, no jewelry. I don't believe that baseball players should look like female movie stars. I've seen some of these guys—they wear more stuff than Elizabeth Taylor.

I've always thought the bean ball was unfair. A pitcher can throw a hard object capable of killing someone at a guy's head, but if the batter runs out there and tries to hit him with his fist, he's in trouble. I like the Phil Cavarretta approach, I saw him do this: A guy had thrown at him a couple times, so the next pitch he swung the bat but he let it go and the bat went whirling out toward the pitcher's head. The pitcher hit the dirt and Cavarretta went strolling out to retrieve his bat and then he punched the guy. So, I think the batters should throw their bats at pitchers.

If you were walking down the street and you had a bat in your hand and a stranger threw a rock at your head you'd probably take the bat and try to hit him, wouldn't you? Well, it makes sense—it's only fair. I think batters should be able to throw their bats at pitchers. That would even it out.

The star players are worth the money because it's like a top salesman. If you got a company and your salesman brings in money you pay 'em because of the business he brings in. But you don't necessarily pay a copy clerk or a file clerk a lot more money because the salesman is doing a good job. We've got bench guys who are knocking down a million dollars a year, really second rate players.

It's not the money, in my case it's the nomadic patterns of ball players. The whole idea of Stan Musial a Cardinal, Marty Marion a Cardinal and Ernie Banks being a Cub for ever and ever—poor bastard didn't deserve that. But the idea of growing up with a team, having a sense that this is your team, these are your players. I don't even know who's playing where, I can't keep up with it. You have to really devote about half of your life to keep track if you're a real baseball fan to study all of these rosters to figure out who's playing where. There's no sense of loyalty. It's all transient, and that's the greatest loss in baseball. It's not the money, it's the transient nature of the players.

Greg Maddux came to the Cubs out of the minor leagues, developed here, the fans had genuine affection for him, he was a hero. Bam, he went off to Atlanta. He didn't understand why he was booed in Chicago. They offered him about the same amount of dough to play here as Atlanta offered him. The Cub management made him more than a fair offer. The average fan feels, what the hell, we cheered you all these years, suddenly you're pitching against us.

I had some tax consultants and financial planners figure out what his contract represented. The guy will be knocking down, if he invests properly, probably half a million dollars a year the rest of his life, even if his arm goes dead. The money at times becomes kind of secondary when you get into those big numbers.

What's wrong with baseball? I don't think expansion. There are enough good athletes around to stock teams. It's the transient nature of the players. They're gypsies now. If you asked me who Reggie Jackson played for during his career, I couldn't tell you.

I know he was with Oakland and the Yankees, but then it gets kind of jumbled up.

But I sure as hell know who Teddy Williams played for and Stan Musial. And Mickey Mantle. Ryne Sandberg; it's unusual that a guy of his quality would be with one team for his whole career. For other people the money may bother them more. The money doesn't bother me that much, unless a guy dogs it.

Trades were kind of fun [as a youngster]. Trades were kind of dramatic things and they weren't that common. Blockbuster trades were fun. Now, guys just pack up, they leave, they go play here, they go play there. If I go out to the ball game I really can't get excited about cheering for Candy Maldonado. I don't know if he will be there when I go to the next ball game.

I happened to like the present Cub team, because we've got several young guys who look like they'll be around here for a while. You'll see them develop; they all look like pretty good ballplayers. So for two or three years they'll be around, but as soon as they get to arbitration, or whatever position they're in, bam, they're liable to be gone. Free agency and they're gone.

ROBERT **LIPSYTE**

e thinks baseball has changed to where it is not going to have the same place in our life it once had. He believes rapid technological advances will put more emphasis on interactive television. There will be smaller live audiences; it will become more of a studio sport. Gambling will become more prevalent.

It sounds depressing as hell to me. Much of baseball's charm comes from being low-tech. The trinity of father, son and baseball might be replaced by software, computer and television.

Robert Lipsyte is a sport columnist for the *New York Times*, author and television producer.

You once wrote an article for Esquire *entitled "The Dying Game." Let me quote the first paragraph:*

> *"The genius of baseball is this: It has so far survived the swine who own it, the clods who manage it, the thugs who play it and amazingly, the Lost Boys of Literature who have tried to love it to death. But silent springs beckon; the Baseball Century is ending. The bats are hollow, the stitches on the ball unravel, the gloves rot. Baseball has become just another enterprise zone of the American soul."*

It's the cycle of history. People talk about the Roman and British Empire and now the American Century being over. Baseball has so inextricably been bound up with the American psyche that the fact that baseball could be coming to an end, which of course doesn't mean it's going to disappear, merely means it's not going to have the same place in our national life that it once had; sounds scarier than it is. I think it's an end to an aspect of history.

I think that we're seeing ourselves go off on small, winnable wars to buck up our self-esteem. We're seeing ourselves not really taking care of business in our inner cities and in the everyday life of this country. So there's a very good chance that baseball is a mirror or an early warning system of American culture, that it could be reflecting what's happening in the larger culture.

Different people think that the game died at different times. The game itself is not dead. The game itself will never die. I don't think anybody in his right mind would say the game is dead. I think that *their* game is dead. *Cheap* baseball is dead. *White* baseball is dead. *Day* baseball is dead. A lot of things that people have taken for granted as theirs, as their birthright, are dead in America.

There's a very good chance that baseball never did live in the fantasy way that we thought. A lot of people think that once baseball was given that anti-trust exemption it should have assumed a heightened responsibility or civic obligation, which it never did. If a game is tacitly allowed to merchandise itself as the national pastime, then this game has a certain obligation to at least . . . at the very least . . . not stick a gun to the head of communities and say, "Build me a domed stadium or I'm outta here."

I don't know that it was illegitimate for O'Malley and Stoneham to move from New York out West. It was the national pastime—why shouldn't it be national? Why shouldn't there be teams in California? I think it's very possible that fans in the East were not supporting those two teams. But somewhere along the line it became an owner tactic of either moving for a better deal or blackmailing a city into giving him a better deal or he would move. Maybe that's when it began to die. I don't think it began to die when the performers, the people who go out and play for us, asked for more money. I'm in a minority here, but I think they probably don't get enough money. No owner has gone broke paying his players.

I think the Yankees are probably the only national baseball team we have; baseball is so regional. But there were Yankee eras. Each was epitomized by a personality.

Babe Ruth in effect saved the game after the Black Sox scandal: The first ballplayer to be sold for a really big price to pay off his owner's debts in other areas, and then come to New York and created this wonderful and exciting legend. He made the game celebrity-driven, big-time, money for everybody and lots of excitement and fantasy.

Joe DiMaggio. He brought something else. His performance and elegance and the sweep of the immigrant waves that were coming into America. Baseball and crime were two of the quickest ways to become Americanized. Joe DiMaggio became an American the honest way.

Mickey Mantle. He was the last white sports hero. It's amazing, I always found him kind of a narrow, suspicious, nasty guy. But he received this terrific press as this kind of last vestige of rural America. "The Natural"—this Sir Galahad.

Jim Bouton is the best sportswriter baseball ever had. *Ball Four* was a wonderful look at the locker room that no journalist had ever given us before. I think it was willfully misread; it was a real valentine. There was a generation of ballplayers after Bouton who read the book when they were in junior high school and high school and said, "I'm going to be a major leaguer." It really turned them on.

George Steinbrenner changed the game and he tapped into that ugly, yuppie, avaricious aspect of America. A greedy, publicity-driven, insecure control freak.

I have a lot of friends who are in Rotisserie League and I don't feel comfortable putting them down, but there's something about Rotisserie League. It started in New York at La Rotisserie restaurant. Rotisserie Leagues are these fantasy leagues in which people buy ballplayers for anywhere from 25 cents to $2.00 at the beginning of the season, and these are players from all the different rosters. You might have "Phalen's Phenoms" in a league of ten or twelve of your friends. Each of you have paid maybe a couple of hundred dollars to buy players and stock your teams. You might have a first baseman from the Yankees and an outfielder from the Blue Jays. Each day you look for certain performance statistics, how your ballplayers did that day. Based on that you can come up with a mathematical figure as to how your team did. Then in the course of the season somebody wins. People become very, very passionate about their teams. That's why it's possible to go to a ballpark and somebody is cheering for a third baseman on one team and a pitcher on the other.

This has in a way objectified the ballplayers into markers in a kind of monopoly game. It really has nothing to do with them being people or skilled athletes. It shifts the fantasy from thinking of yourself as a player to imagining yourself an owner, as someone who has contracts on all this flesh out there.

I wouldn't go so far as to say it's alarming, or it's going to be the end of western civilization as we know it, but it certainly is a turn in the way we see ourselves in society and the way we see our games and entertainments.

You have a Three Point Plan for saving baseball. The first point is to give back childhood.

I feel most strongly about that. My son played Little League. My daughter was in other sports, but while I'm not so innocent as to think that you can just throw a ball out on a vacant lot for kids to play the way they did when I was a kid—I'm not so sure that that doesn't lead to "Lord of the Flies" sports anyway—but, I think that kids are oversupervised, overcoached, overpressured in situations that have absolutely no value at that age. I think that Little League in the way it has become a kind of grotesque midget replica of the major leagues is a way to stunt childhood. I would cancel Little League. I don't think it has any value in its present form except to ruin self-esteem and pitching arms. We've seen too much disaster and corruption. It stinks.

Second, whether cities should be major league or not. My biggest concern there is that in many ways bringing in a major league team to a city in trouble is really like cosmeticizing a corpse. I've been on some of these owners' conventions where delegations come from cities with their proposals and their money begging for an expansion franchise. I've heard people that I wanted to respect—judges, important politicians, leading business people—say a city is not major league until it has a major league team. Forget about hospitals, infrastructure, police, education— just give us a major league team. Stick us on the "happy news network" and we'll get investment possibilities and we'll be able to be good someday. I can't be a statesman until I get elected; right now I'm just a politician. My proposal is, let these teams be major league or not, depending on their performance.

Third is a moratorium on stories about athletes except what they do between the white lines. Too much of it is fawning, sickening . . . what a great New York editor, Stanley Woodward, once called "godding up" the ballplayers. Most of them are limited simply because from the age of twelve they've been channeled into this and they're very narrow. But a lot of surgeons are very narrow, too, and a lot of other specialists are narrow. That's okay. For a while at least, let's talk about what they do. Let's deal with the performance. This is not a hard and fast point like the first two, just an attempt to step away and let some of the gas out of this bag.

I was living in New York in '57 when the two teams went west. Since I was a Yankee fan, it was no ice pick in my heart. But it was a time of tremendous discussion and re-evaluation; soul-searching and a lot of stuff was in the air that we had never dealt with before. Nobody is as parochial as New Yorkers. We knew everything. We were in our own little world. We had three teams and they might as well have been the whole major league. Then all of a sudden two of them went away and the first thought is, *Whoa, is something wrong with us? We're not good enough?* It was a period of enormous discussion and evaluation.

I think baseball is going to remain as a game, but I think it's going to become more and more of a studio sport. It will be played in domed stadiums, to smaller and smaller live audiences. That's going to matter less and less as games are going to be seen pay-per-view. I think you'd be very hard put to find a game that would lend itself so well to sports gambling through the course of a game.

Once there's interactive television you're going to be able to hit a keyboard in front of you. I see a future where you're going to be watching a game on your combination television set-computer. You're going to be sitting in front of a keyboard. The technology now exists for interactive television. Within a few years they'll start with a few games whereby four or five times during the course of a game the action will be stopped and the announcer will say, "You folks at home can now make a decision. Should we put in a new pitcher? Shall we put in a new hitter?" You can tap into your keyboard "yes" or "no," or whatever permutations are available. In a sense then, fans will become managers for a few plays in the course of a game to incite interest.

Nine people will still be out there playing baseball, but with the enormous psychic changes, the fantasy changes, it will no way be the game that you know. You will say and I will say, "Baseball is dead, our baseball is dead." But our children, or our children's children playing this game, this Nintendo baseball game with live people, will say, "You're crazy. It's never been so exciting." And they may well be right.

VIN **SCULLY**

R ed Barber hired Vin in 1950 to work the Brooklyn Dodger games with him. This was heady stuff for a 22-year-old fresh out of college.

Barber gave him some advice he has always adhered to: Don't get close to the players, and always be yourself. In fact, he never listens to other announcers in an effort to maintain his own style.

Vin Scully doesn't need to listen to anyone else. He is the best to ever broadcast baseball. He is an American original.

After I graduated college I went to work for CBS in Washington for WTOP which was, and is, a 50,000-watt station, so it was in a sense the equivalent of going from college to the major leagues. I was a summer replacement announcer and they offered me a permanent job come the spring. I worked there from May to October and they said, "Good luck, stay well, and we'll see you in March" and I said, "Great."

I had a couple of letters of introduction, one of which was to Red Barber, and I chatted with him and I left my name and phone number. A couple of days later when I came home my red-haired Irish mother, highly excitable, said, "You'll never guess who called," and I said "Who?" and she said, "Red Skelton." I said, "No, I don't think so, but how about Red Barber?" Anyway, I called Red. There was an emergency, a shortage of one announcer to fill out the hand for the *CBS Football Round-Up,* a show on radio. They did four football games, not simultaneously, but would bounce from game to game and they were short an announcer. Ernie Harwell was given the Notre Dame-North Carolina game in New York. I was given Boston University and Maryland in Boston. The Notre Dame game fell apart; Charlie Justice was an All-American with North Carolina, he was injured very early, Notre Dame won easily. The other games suddenly lacked interest, they were one-sided, and I had a super game. My game ended one point difference, the down team driving, being caught on the eight yard line; very, very exciting.

When I had gotten to Boston I assumed everything would be great because I'm working for the network. But when I got there I wound up with a microphone and fifty yards of cable, and I was on the roof of the ballpark, running up and down Fenway and looking down trying to broadcast the football game, while moving as much as the players. Luckily for me I never said anything about my problems. Red got a letter of apology from the people in Boston; this made what was no doubt a very ordinary job in his mind suddenly somewhat extraordinary, that a kid could do an ordinary job under those circumstances. He called me and said, "Don't worry, you'll have a booth next week, you're doing Harvard-Yale." That was a big feather in my cap and shortly thereafter I got another call from him to be in his office, and that's when Ernie Harwell had moved over to the Giants and that began the first step in the direction of baseball.

Red Barber, Connie Desmond and myself did all the games at home and twenty-five on the road [for Brooklyn]. So there were 102 games that were on radio and television. They needed a third man and I fell into the category and I did a couple of innings— I usually did the third and the seventh on radio and filled in once in a while on television.

Red left in '53. Connie Desmond was still there, bless his heart. But Connie had all kinds of problems, and so eventually because of his problems I became the number one announcer.

The "boys of summer" were kind of my graduating class. In other words, I started with them. I suffered for them, all their frustrating years of '50, '51 and '52. I did the World Series in '53, but they couldn't make that. When they finally won it in '55, the combination that it was their first and I was still relatively young and wide-eyed made the impact overwhelming.

I was as young as the youngest player, so I really didn't have anyone to hang out with. The writers were older, Red and Connie were much older, so Red warned me not to gravitate the way he knew I would go—to fellows my own age. So I pretty much kept to myself, or with Allen Roth who was then the Dodgers' statistician, and it was a good bit of advice because I did not allow emotion or friendship to color a description.

The other thing, he was well aware of Mel Allen, Russ Hodges, all the wonderful announcers back there, and he told me not to listen to anyone else. He said, "You bring something into the booth that no one else can bring." I looked at him and said, "Well, what in the world can that be?" He said, "Yourself."

So I have never listened, even to this day, and any expression that I have, anything that I say or do is mine, because I don't listen to anybody else. Admittedly, I could learn from other people, but I go back to Red saying, "Don't take the risk of watering your own wine."

I remember the Dodgers' move very well, and I was somewhat afraid. After all, I had an affinity with New York because for the first time I was "one of them" who made it to the booth. The broadcasting booths in New York were full of southerners, and all of a sudden here's a kid from the streets of New York doing play-by-play, and I think the people were extremely kind to me in the early going because of that. Now suddenly we're uprooting and coming to California and I was a little leery of whether I would do as well in California as I was doing in New York. But fortunately, things worked out.

First of all, the games were played in a football stadium, the Coliseum. Secondly, the fans were well aware of the superstars, but they weren't aware of the rank and file. The timing was perfect for me to talk about all these players because the transistor radio came into being. So I was very fortunate—it wasn't me. It was all of the other circumstances put together and I just happened to be the one to profit from it.

*The difference between Brooklyn and Los Angeles must have been
like night and day.*

Well, it was. First of all, the actual ballpark was as different as
the communities they represented. Ebbets Field was very small,
very, very intimate, very personal. The fans had a longstanding
feeling for the ball club because it represented them. People
always made fun of the people in Brooklyn and they resented it.
So any success the team had made the people in the borough
feel better. They were made fun of in the movies; people always
had this horrible Brooklyn accent, etc. When we came to Los
Angeles, in a sense, there was somewhat the same feeling. Where
Brooklyn felt that New Yorkers looked down on them, Angelenos
felt that San Francisco looked down on them. So the success of
the ball club united the city and gave them something to be proud
of in the early going.

You could say the competition might not be as sharp as it was,
and that makes sense because we've gone from eight teams to
sixteen and it's pretty hard to maintain all of the competitiveness
and the quality of an eight-team league.

I'll give you another idea. When I started with the Brooklyn
Dodgers and went to spring training we had twenty-six minor
league teams. Now, I think, we have four. Now what that means
is, sure there's only an additional three hundred players in the
big leagues, but there's an awful lot of players who are not truly
prepared who are playing in the big leagues. They have not spent
seven, eight years in the minor leagues to really sharpen up. So
there's a difference in the overall quality, absolutely.

We have kids making it today that—it's on-the-job training.
They're learning to play in the big leagues while in the big
leagues. In the old days they learned the fundamentals and it took
them a long time before they got here. I really think the change
starts in the minor leagues.

The coaches and the managers in the big leagues today have
a completely different job than they used to have. Today, they
have to be teachers. In the old days the teachers were in the
minor leagues, and then they came up and played.

You know, the older you get you realize that you pay a *tremendous* price in being in the game. And sure, we're well-paid and there's fame and all the other stuff that goes with it. But the price is this: The most precious thing that we have outside of good health is time. And yet, when you're on the road you spend most of your time "killing" that precious thing. You're away from your family, you're away from your children and you are just looking at the clock. Waiting to get to the ballpark, and as you get older that weighs heavier and heavier.

Once I'm seated behind the microphone, once the game begins, I'm totally immersed in it and I love the game and I enjoy watching it played. As soon as the game is over, then that mood sets in again and it stays with you until the anthem of the following game.

The Dodgers had a pitcher named Russ Meyer. He was traded from the Phillies to the Dodgers in 1953. Meyer had said in the winter, something to the effect, "If I can't win eighteen games with the Dodgers I ought to hang it up. It will be good to leave the Phillies because they don't score very many runs." And this enraged the people in Philadelphia. The Dodgers came to Philadelphia for their first weekend series and Dressen had announced that Russ Meyer was going to pitch. Connie Mack Stadium was *jammed* to capacity and the crowd booed him while he was warming up, and by the time the game started Meyer was furious and the fans were all over him. And being angry,he was less effective and they got some walks and then a base hit, another walk, and he started to holler at the umpire, and before you know it he is on the ropes. They've got a couple of runs, they've got men on base. And here comes Charley Dressen and Meyer is so furious that he bends down and picks up the rosin bag and throws the rosin bag as high in the air as you can humanly throw a rosin bag, and with his arms folded he just glared at the approaching Dressen and the rosin bag came down and hit him right on top of the head.

It was unbelievable that you could throw a rosin bag so high and then have it come down and hit you on the head. And of course he had that Dodger blue hat and all of a sudden it was covered with rosin. That was one in a million.

You mentioned the "boys of summer." There aren't many left.

Sooner or later, it's going to happen to all of us. So I can certainly put it in perspective. So far, it's been Hodges, Robinson, Reese, Cox, Campanella and Walker, the catchers. Furillo and Amoros in the outfield, Don Drysdale, the pitcher, and Walter Alston, the manager, along with Charley Dressen. So, they're gone and I'm a much richer person for having known them.

GERALD **ESKENAZI**

Pee Wee Reese said Leo Durocher was possibly the only manager people paid to see manage. Leo was arrogant, abrasive,
bright, knowledgeable, intuitive and a winner. He had many ene-
mies but no one said he was a fool. His players respected him, as did
baseball people. As a manager he won 2,008 games, placing him seventh in total wins, but only recently was inducted into the Hall of
Fame. This might be the price he paid for being a pain in the ass.

Gerald Eskenazi is the author of *The Lip*, a biography of Leo
Durocher. He is a sports writer for the *New York Times*.

To understand Leo and his self-promotion, his grandiose way
of living and dressing, you had to understand that he came from
a troubled family background. His father was one of those that
at the first of the month would disappear. His mother took in
boarders and he spent a lot of his life on the streets of West
Springfield, Massachusetts. He early on became a pool hustler and
a card shark and he really almost lived by his wits. Very engag-
ing young man who everyone liked in West Springfield. When
he was 15 or 16 he already had his eyes on the expensive suit
in the store window that he couldn't afford. He would hop from
being an altar boy in church, to running across the street and
stealing doughnuts from the bakery. He was really a contradic-
tory sort of person.

He had absolutely no talent as a hitter. But he was considered
maybe the best fielder of his time at short which he developed
when he was at Cincinnati. With the Yankees he never was really
more than a sixty percent or seventy percent-of-the-time player.

With Cincinnati, and then of course with the "Gas House Gang"
Cardinals, he was the anchor of that infield and very often pro-
tected Frankie Frisch, who was getting older and slower at second base. People that played alongside him said he was
absolutely the smartest player they had ever seen.

He was almost from his rookie days with the Yankees a con-
tentious ballplayer. In fact, would often razz Babe Ruth on the
bench, claiming he was slow and telling him to stop complaining and moaning. He also was the apple of Miller Huggins' eye.
He took after Huggins. Huggins gave him his head, saw that he
was a smart player who, like Huggins, was smallish, scrappy and
with limited talent. He told Leo that they could use their brains
and they'd always be better than the big galoots that baseball
seemed to have.

In fact, when he took over as manager of the Dodgers he said
that he was sorry that Huggins could not be there. He took
Huggins' style. Huggins, of course, with "Murderer's Row" didn't
need to do a lot of intelligent baseball.

He certainly didn't screw it up when he had good clubs. It's
very hard to figure a manager's impact. What you say about managers is the old cliché: "If you have the horses . . ." His greatest
managing feat came in '51 where the Giants were 13½ back of
the Dodgers and went on to win. That was one of the really great
managing feats. He certainly did make a difference. He probably
would have won another pennant in '47 with the Dodgers when
he was suspended just a few days before the season opened. On
the other hand, who knows if the Dodgers' demise in '48 might
have been to some degree his fault because of his rancorous relationship with Jackie Robinson. Who knows to what degree the
'69 Chicago Cubs collapse. I'm sure, in retrospect, a lot of the
players blame him. I'm not sure it is quite that simple.

You can't knock success. In other words, everyone that wins
a pennant has great players. Look at Sparky Anderson, look at
the Yankee managers. But the point is you don't know what
someone else would have done. You do know what they did with
the manager who was there. I have to credit him for a winning

percentage of .540, which is pretty good.

He took certain players under his wing. Pete Reiser, Willie Mays, Eddie Stanky and Sal Maglie come to mind. He had a guy in '45 named Tom Seats who had a drinking problem. Durocher would get him half tight before a game and the guy had a 10-7 record that year. Never played again. He had a way of working with some ballplayers and being a pain in the ass to others.

It was strictly based on how ballplayers would react to the way he handed down his judgments. He gave Pee Wee Reese a terrible time because he didn't like rookies in some cases, and yet look how he handled Willie Mays ten years later. Pee Wee Reese came up as a rookie in 1940 and he kept benching Pee Wee and kept on him. I think it was just part of the impenetrable personality and impenetrable shell that Leo Durocher had. It's a mystery how he could have players love him and have so many hate him. How he could be on the one hand so patient in '51, and so edgy in '69—but you know Leo was a man of contradictions. Not having majored in psychiatry, I don't think I could really explain it other than he was a guy who managed by the seat of his pants. Very often he was right, as with the drunks. Very often with rookies he was wrong, and sometimes with rookies, like with Willie Mays, he helped make him the greatest player of his time.

He thought Willie was absolutely the greatest player. When you think about the great hitters in baseball history you think of them with a bat in their hand. You don't think of them on the base paths, catching fly balls or running. The image of Willie could be any one of those and I think that's why he really liked him. Willie was a very, very smart ballplayer.

As far as pitchers are concerned, it was Maglie and Freddie Fitzsimmons. He liked their ability to win in the clutch. He also liked Maglie's record against the Dodgers. Maglie, Fitzsimmons, and Mays were players that he really admired. He admired their talent as well as their smarts in the game.

In 1947, before the season started, Durocher was suspended for the season and put under "sentence of silence" by the commissioner, Happy Chandler. What happened? Why was he suspended?

Actually, many reasons. It was what Chandler called a "culmination of unpleasant incidents." What had happened was in the previous two or three years Chandler had been getting phone calls from many people whom Durocher owed money, including, believe it or not, Bill "Bo Jangles" Robinson, the tap dancer. In '45 Leo had beaten up a fan under the stands at Ebbets Field with the help of a special security guard, who also acted as Leo's bodyguard. Leo defied the courts by marrying Laraine Day, a well-known actress of the time while her American divorce wasn't official. He married her in Mexico. He usually and regularly consorted with gamblers. The last straw was 1947 when he complained in a ghostwritten column he had in the *Brooklyn Eagle* that Larry MacPhail, his old nemesis and former boss on the Dodgers, now the Yankees' general manager, was himself consorting with gamblers and had gamblers in his box in training camp in Havana.

The funny thing is those two gamblers were also friends of Durocher's! So now in the public's mind they have these two gamblers, and they have Durocher, and they think that Leo was suspended for gambling in 1947. Because he made the complaints about MacPhail and these two gamblers being entertained by MacPhail in public, Chandler saw fit to call him into a private hearing in Florida and complained that this was not in the so-called umbrella of "the best interests of baseball." So Leo Durocher ultimately got kicked out, not for gambling himself, but for complaining about someone else's gambling, complaining about someone else's associates. But it really was a combination of things, it wasn't just the one thing. Chandler subsequently said that he felt he had to do it because Leo was in a downward spiral—gambling, associating with gamblers, his marriage, beating fans up, not paying off his gambling debts. He felt that he would never recover and this one year would give him a chance to remove himself. Get him out of the public eye and let him clean up his act.

Harrold Parrott actually wrote the article.

He told Parrott about it, Parrott wrote it, and Leo, to his credit never backed down from it. Leo never wrote a word of it. I'm not even sure he read it. But he didn't back down from it which as a newspaperman I respect. Because ballplayers and other athletes very often say, "Oh, I didn't say this," or "I didn't say that."

The Giants were not a Cinderella team in 1951. They became a Cinderella team because they were down so much and came back. It wasn't like the 1969 Mets coming from nowhere. In fact, the Giants for the last five weeks of 1950 had the best record in baseball. They were coming on very strong and in the 1951 *Sporting News,* in a pre-season poll, the Giants were picked to win the National League pennant over the Dodgers despite the Dodgers' Hall of Fame contingent going for them.

I remember it—I was a Dodger fan. I remember giving three-to-one odds when the Dodgers had an eight or a ten game lead that they would beat the Giants and I remember losing three bucks. And like everyone else, I remember what I was doing at three minutes to four when Thomson hit the home run.

It was a special time. It's probably difficult for fans who 1) are not that old and 2) fans who do not have two teams in the same city. Comparable to UCLA-USC playing each other four times a year. Or Iowa-Iowa State or Michigan-Michigan State playing each other. Not only playing each other, but imagine their head coach jumping from one club to the other in mid-season? When Durocher jumped from the Dodgers to the Giants in 1948 the Dodgers were winning the season series against the Giants. The rest of that season, the Giants won their remaining part of the season series against the Dodgers. He was immediately booed—not only in Ebbets Field, but in the Polo Grounds where they hated him.

He and Jackie Robinson did not get along. When Leo was managing them in '47, before his suspension, he found out in Havana that Dixie Walker was circulating a petition to the southern-born players to boycott the games and, in fact, to ask to be traded. They didn't want Jackie Robinson. Leo found out about it after Dixie Walker had dinner with one of his assistants, and his assistant immediately called Leo—he found out about it at midnight. At midnight, Leo summoned most of the ballplayers on the team to the kitchen of the hotel. And at 1:00 A.M., Leo, in his pajamas, spoke to all the players and told them that if there was any guy that would not play with Jackie Robinson, they were going to be gone. He felt that Jackie Robinson was going to be a great ballplayer, put money in their pockets. He said, "I don't know about you, but I like to eat a good steak." And then, of course, three or four days before the season began Leo was suspended for the year so he never managed Jackie Robinson that first year. Although as they went North and had to play in southern cities that had never had black players and white players together, he helped integrate them when there were several instances of ballparks that refused them access to the white players' entrance, etc. He insisted that Robinson dress with the Dodgers.

So in '48, Leo is really angry and obsessed with not having managed in '47. Burt Shotton leads this team to the pennant and they take the Yankees to seven games, and Leo was convinced he could have won the pennant and the World Series with the '47 Dodgers. Training camp starts and Jackie isn't around. Jackie, it turns out, was making his life story, his movie, in which he starred, so he was in Hollywood. He didn't get to training camp until three days after training camp starts so Leo is fuming. Robinson shows up and Leo is shocked; Jackie had put on twenty-five pounds in the off-season from all those dinners and speaking engagements. This lean, hard Jackie Robinson, who led the league in stolen bases as a rookie, hit .297, had this sensational season, shows up fat. Now he's fat Jackie Robinson. Leo is furious with him and felt that he never really got out of Robinson what he should have.

Now it's mid-season and the Dodgers are floundering and he switches to the Giants. As a Jackie Robinson opponent he has the opportunity to razz him and scream at him, which he does. The two went at it forever after that. Jackie, at this point would not back down, and of course, in '49 and '50 he was even more outspoken and Leo, of course, with his big mouth. So the two of them always went at it. Jackie was a symbol of the Dodgers. He eventually became their leader—not their captain; Pee Wee was the captain. Leo was always the symbol of the Giants. That was the genesis of their hatred for each other.

He quit the Giants at the end of the 1955 season, the Giants finishing third that year. What did he do until he went with the Cubs in 1966?

He did several things. He went on television. He was the host of an NBC daily show called *Matinee Theater.* I think he even tried a little acting in it. He was also a one- or two-time host of the *Colgate Comedy Hour.* He did some work for one of the networks on *The Game of the Week.* He did a lot of speaking. But he really was not in baseball at all. Laraine taught him the finer points of life. They did a lot of traveling together. He became an art collector and a collector of objects of art. He had become sort of a national personality and always played his character. He always played this loud talking brash guy.

From 1966 to more than halfway through the '72 season he managed the Cubs, leaving to go to Houston.

He was considered a pain in the ass by then. He had become even more of a braggart. Norm Miller, one of the ballplayers on the Astros in those days said they were playing cards when Leo joined the club and someone said to him, "Boy, those are nice boots." He had snakeskin boots or alligator boots. He said, "They're from Frank's bootmaker." Frank, of course, is Sinatra. Norm Miller said the guys replied, "Oh, don't give us that Frank shit, Leo, where do you think you are? You're not back in New York now." He said it was a bunch of guys that really were very compatible and liked each other and Leo came in as an irritant in this whole mix. And I guess one of the reasons they didn't like him was that they didn't win as much as they should have.

Here was a guy playing on artificial turf, under artificial lighting. Some years before he had complained about the Astrodome, complained about the lighting and tore the phone out in anger, claiming that it wasn't a fit ballpark for baseball and did not like artificial turf. He was 67 years old at the time, so the symbolism of Leo Durocher winding up on Astroturf was just more than he could bear at that point.

But then again, they still played over .500 for him. Despite his age and despite everything else, they still had a decent record.

Marvin Miller details how,as part of the collective bargaining agreement, he was permitted to address every team in baseball, to update them on the current union rulings, union salaries and the status of life. This particular day he had them (the Astros) before an exhibition game, meeting in center field. He said, "All of a sudden I heard some noises behind me. I looked around and there were balls dropping behind me. Leo was out near home plate laughing." He had directed his coaches to hit fungoes out to center field. What the ballplayers did was surround Marvin Miller, protecting him from all those bouncing balls.

Later that day Miller lodged a formal complaint with the National League President, Charles Feeney, and in fact was going to go to the National Labor Relations Board and make a "federal case" out of it. Feeney headed him off by 1) talking to Durocher and 2) fining him. I don't know how much it was; it was in the thousands of dollars.

He retired in 1973. By then he was 68 and he became a sort of celebrity. He did card shows, especially with his good buddy Willie Mays. Whenever he needed a few thousand dollars he would do some card stuff. He also had several affairs with women in his later years. In fact, about five years after that, when he was about 73 years old, he was dating a woman in New York about 30 years old and he had a penile implant attempt. I spoke to the nurse that was sort of his private nurse and she said that the procedure was paid for by Sinatra.

He led a sort of bon vivant life after that. He and Sinatra jet-setted all over the world. Frank had a private fleet of jets. He also became very friendly with the "Rat Pack" and would go with them to Vegas. Dated younger women. He had married a Chicago television personality, Lynn Walker Goldblatt. They eventually divorced. He was always needing money from her and then in his later years he had become very bitter.

He died in October '91. He was admitted to the hospital on the anniversary of Bobby Thomson's home run. He was frail by then and had been injured in a car accident about a year earlier. He was bitter about life and a lot of his joy seemed to have left him, a lot of his exuberance. But he was also 86 years old.

LARRY **GERLACH**

Professor of Early American History and Sport History at the University of Utah, he has devoted years to the study of baseball umpiring. His book *Men In Blue* deals with the subject.

To my knowledge, baseball has never been played or umpired strictly to the letter of the rule book. Never. There are few absolutes in a rule book; the vast majority of the rules are judgmental. So over the passage of time umpires in various professional leagues have, on the direction of league administrators, and with the suggestions of coaches and players, established variable strike zones.

The "phantom double play" at second base: People were getting hurt with players sliding hard into the bag and so it became a matter of accepted play that the second baseman on a play that is not particularly close doesn't have to touch the bag.

If an infielder makes an exceptional effort and makes an outstanding play the batter is out regardless of whether he may have just barely beaten the throw. The good play is rewarded with the proper call.

Baseball is not unique in that respect. I'm somewhat amazed that people who watch football and basketball understand that officials are not officiating a game strictly according to the rule book, but using their judgment in what is allowable or not. But people seem to be either unaware or unwilling to accept that in baseball. No sport is officiated strictly by the rule book.

If you start out in the Rookie Leagues the strike zone is very big all the way around. Up, down, inside, outside. If you called it strictly by the book in the Rookie Leagues no pitcher would ever throw strikes. As you move up through the minor leagues the strike zone gets smaller and smaller and smaller. Umpires know that, players know that, managers know that. Everybody knows that. League officials demand that.

If you have a pitcher who is wild, he's going to have to throw the ball right down the middle to get a strike. A pitcher who has very good control and is consistently placing the ball a couple inches off the plate is going to get the strike calls. He's putting the ball where he wants to put it. The batter knows that. The pitcher knows that. Everybody knows that. An erratic pitcher without good control is not going to get that kind of leeway.

Which are the hardest calls for an umpire?

There are four. One is a checked swing where even now that call is made on appeal to either a first base or third base umpire, but it's still called different from the rule book. The rule is it doesn't make any difference if the batter goes all the way around or not, he ceases swinging at the ball when he stops making an effort to hit it. But that's not how they call it. They call it on the basis of how far the bat goes over the plate. That's a tough one for a plate umpire. And it's a tough one for the base umpires, too, 'cause they don't have a good perspective.

Another is a hit batsman where a ball just barely hits the batter or hits the batter and the bat almost simultaneously. It's very hard and the umpire will almost always key off the reaction of the batter as to whether he got hit or not.

Third tough call is a trapped ball in the outfield. With four umpires it's much easier than it used to be with three. But it still can be a real problem.

And the most difficult decision of all is for an umpire to throw a player or a manager out of the game when the umpire knows he kicked the call.

Who have been some of the famous umpire baiters?

The worst of all time was John McGraw. He was awful with umpires. McGraw was just an acerbic, unhappy jerk. He was hell on umpires and really everybody else in his life, except his wife and Christy Mathewson. Other than those two, he was a miserable human being. Durocher was terrible and Earl Weaver is probably the worst of modern times. I would say Earl Weaver and John McGraw are the two worst.

McGraw and Weaver were attempting to do two things. One, they created an act for show, and that's really annoying to umpires and players and everybody concerned. It's part of their persona. Part of the way they go about doing business.

The other part is they're trying to divert attention from the inadequacies or mistakes of their players by shunting the blame or the attention on the umpire. There were some umpire baiters— Durocher and Billy Martin—who didn't really get under the umpires' skin all that much because that was a reflection of their personality, their competitiveness and their psychological short fuses. Billy Martin was just Billy Martin and everybody knew that. There was a phoniness about what Earl Weaver and John McGraw did which made their behavior more difficult to tolerate.

Most people would say Bill Klem was the best umpire. I would personally rank Bill McGowan first, Al Barlick second and then probably Klem and Connolly for third and fourth.

There are hundreds and hundreds of people that umpired one year or two and were gone. Once somebody's in the major leagues for more than two or three years then they're good umpires. It's like a ballplayer. If a baseball player stays in the major leagues more than two years the odds are overwhelming that that player is going to be there nine or ten years. That's a good baseball player. The vast majority of players don't last more than two years. I don't have a sense of any particular umpire or umpires being year-in and year-out described formally or informally as bad umpires.

They ran Pallone out because he was homosexual. There's no question about that. One year he would not be ranked very high and the next year he would be ranked fairly high. And he's typical. He had certain years in which things happened and he went off half-cocked, the Pete Rose thing being the classic example of that. But then again he'd come back and he was very good.

Pallone was an average umpire. He wasn't great, he wasn't real bad. If anything, Pallone was probably more erratic than most. I'm not sure why. It's probably because of the psychological pressures that he was feeling. But he was erratic.

Pallone was the first modern umpire about whom there were rumors of homosexuality. Pallone got by with being homosexual, in the sense of not being detected, because he was one of the "scab" umps. Normally, their private lives are pretty open. Given the exaggerated macho dimension of athletics I think it would be exceedingly difficult for a gay umpire not to be identified almost immediately. Without Pallone being a "scab," it would have come to the surface many years before.

It was social ostracism. They never associated with him. Umpires tend to hang together, but not with Pallone and the other "scabs." They literally lived alone so Pallone was able to do whatever it was he was doing without the scrutiny of the group.

Up until the fifties, it's a common occurrence for umpires to be physically abused in the minor leagues. One of the problems we have with baseball is that when people talk about baseball they're not really talking about baseball. They're talking about major league baseball which is a very, very small component of baseball. So the whole minor league experience is one of consistent physical abuse, threatening abuse of umpires well into the 1950s.

There've been half a dozen or more women umpires. Pam Postema went further than anyone else. She got to AAA.

I think they bounced her because of gender. I don't know. Her book is pretty good in the sense that she's so candid about herself and what happened to her that you don't know whether she got let go because she was female or because she wasn't a good enough umpire. There's enough evidence for either. She's very candid about her shortcomings as an umpire.

The last time I saw her was in the Pacific Coast League. My sense was that she was very good. Very good behind the plate, not very good on the bases. The bases—that's largely a mechanical thing and can be corrected. The harder assignment is the plate, and she was very good at that. I don't know about her last four to five years. But I thought she certainly, on the basis of what she did behind the plate, had the ability to be a major league umpire.

After retirement some umpires will put the finger on managers. Most of them will say, "Weaver was a real problem. A real pain in the ass." Period. Umpires tend to be very defensive. They tend to be very cliquish. They don't like "kiss and tell" stuff. I've talked to dozens and dozens and they are not likely to talk at any length about managers. It's clear who they don't like and why they don't like 'em, but they're not going to tell stories about them.

Athletes generally don't know the rules. Basketball players don't know the rules. Football players don't know the rules. They couldn't begin to officiate a contest. They wouldn't even know where to stand. Most people who watch sports don't have a clue about the rules either. That makes it very hard for umpires because the players and the fans don't know the rule book, let alone the informal code and interpretation by which the game is actually run. So the official is in a no-win situation. The umpires have a difficult job because they're devoting their lives, their professional careers to something that the players and fans by their basic ignorance are contemptuous of. It's really hard because people don't respect what they're doing. The lack of knowledge about rules is nothing more than a lack of respect for the game, but particularly for the umpires.

I had the opportunity to call balls and strikes at a couple of umpire schools when they used a pitching machine. I literally couldn't tell whether it was a ball or a strike. I made a couple of calls and I was not even close. I am just in awe of anybody who's calling balls and strikes behind the plate. I couldn't call it off a pitching machine.

It's important if people are going to appreciate baseball to watch umpires. For just an inning or two when a ball is hit watch the umpires instead of the ball or the runner to get a sense of what they do. My experience has been when people do that they will never, ever watch baseball again the same way. It opens up a whole other dimension. It changes your sense of the whole thing and makes you appreciate the game a lot more.

THE GRANDSTAND

KEITH **GERST**

hildhood dreams and perceptions are like a strong stain: Once they sink in they are hard to remove. But part of growing up is to shed these dreams and perceptions and get on with the real world. As we all know this can be a painful transition. During the 1946 World Series between the St. Louis Cardinals and Boston Red Sox, Keith Gerst discovered that one of his childhood heroes had feet of clay. It was a tough bump along the road of life.

I have a lot of memories of Old Sportsman's Park in St. Louis. In the 1940s my boyhood chums and I grew up almost in the shadow of that old ballpark. To us it was the center of the universe because it seemed that the Cardinals, led by Stan Musial, were in the thick of every pennant race and World Series that came along. Yeah, I have a lot of memories of those days, but one I'll never forget had to do with a western movie star and the '46 World Series.

My buddies and I, all between the ages of eight and twelve, were hanging around the ball park trying to make a buck anyway we could. I was selling peanuts—fifteen cents a bag—around the old Dodier Street grandstand entrance, when who but Gabby Hayes, Roy Rogers' sidekick, came up to me and bought a couple of bags. I knew *immediately* who he was because Roy Rogers and Gabby Hayes were about as big a heroes to my friends and me as "Stan the Man" and Marty Marion were. A Hollywood western star in St. Louis at a Cardinal game? This was big stuff! I figured Roy was probably waiting for him, because I just knew that they were never apart.

After selling my last bag of peanuts I raced down to the Walgreen Drugstore several blocks away to tell my friends. The drugstore was our meeting place where we drank Cokes and listened to the game on a portable radio. I quickly told my pals what had happened and we excitedly agreed we would wait for Gabby to come out after the game and try to talk to him.

When the game was over five of my friends and I kept watch. Sure enough, here he came. Gabby had a few friends with him, but Roy wasn't one of them. My buddies and I were a little disappointed, but what the heck, we still had Gabby.

We followed him across Grand Avenue and down Dodier Street going to wherever they had parked. "Hey, Gabby! Where's Roy? Gabby, do you have your six-gun? Gabby, where's Dale?" we called out innocently. Gabby seemed to be mumbling answers, but we just couldn't hear him. Finally when Jerry, the youngest of our group, called out again, "Gabby, where's Roy?" we got a response. Gabby whirled around, faced us, paused . . . and then yelled, "Why don't you kids go fuck yourselves!" Jerry looked at me and I looked at Jerry as our little group turned around and in silence walked back towards the ball park. As we walked, Jerry said to no one in particular, "Geez, what did he mean by that?".

Oh, well, that was a long time ago. Time has taught me that everyone in life, whether in baseball or western movies, can have a bad day.

DAVE **FILKIN**

In 1977, Dave played second base for his team in the last three innings for the Wheaton, Illinois Pony League Championship. He had five fielding chances and blew them all. In addition, he was called out on a bunt base hit because he stepped on home plate.

His team lost and he was too upset to receive his second place trophy. Afterward, it seemed to him that all of Wheaton knew of his performance and commented personally to him about it. He has never played a game of baseball since.

Life can be a bitch and so can baseball.

I grew up playing in the Wheaton Little League Park District League and for four straight years I was probably the best guy on my team. Then it was time to go to the Pony Leagues and I got drafted by the White Sox in the Pony League division.

It was late July 1977 and our team was in the championship game. This game was played underneath the lights in front of my soon-to-be high school, Wheaton Central. During that season I was probably one of the worst players on my team. I played second base, and because the rule stood that you had to play at least three innings, I got to play the last three innings of every game at second base. [In] this championship game I go in as usual at the start of the fourth inning. No sooner am I in the game and the first play is a pop-up to me. I call everybody off and the next thing I know the ball has missed my glove but found my head. I can hear the laughing, and of course the guy is safe at first base and I'm a little shaken up.

Two or three batters later I get a ground ball right to me; easy ground ball to field. Next thing I know I'm looking behind me, the ball's out in right field. At least one run scores.

The fifth or sixth batter, another ground ball comes to me—we've got a force at second base. I try to make the play, just flip it to the shortstop covering second base, and I trip and fall and don't get the ball to him. There's probably been six batters and I've created three errors and what little lead we had going into the fourth inning has now dissipated and we're tied or losing by a run. I can hear people chanting, "Hit it to Filkin."

We are in the fifth inning and I get an easy ground ball, field it beautifully. I can still remember getting that ball in my glove, feeling like I have conquered the world; and threw it about three feet over the first baseman. I have one more fielding error, a throw to the shortstop, but it ended up behind the third base dugout. I had five fielding errors.

I can't remember one play that I made good on. It seemed like the whole team was hitting it to me, which doesn't happen very often at second base, which was the reason I was playing second base. We get to the top of the seventh, we're down by a couple runs. I can remember there's a guy on second and my coach, Jim Vivian, gives me the bunt sign. I can remember the pitcher, he was throwing photons. I couldn't have seen the ball if my life depended on it. I lay down a beautiful bunt, get to first base, look back, notice the guy from second standing on third base, we're both safe, until I hear the home plate umpire yell, "You're out." I had stepped on home plate. That's two outs. The next guy up strikes out. We lost the game 9-5, 8-4, whatever. It wasn't even close; we were winning before I got into the game.

I can remember crying unmercifully during the awards ceremony. I got a nice second place trophy and I would not go get it when they called my name. I can still hear people laughing, screaming, going, "That's Filkin, 'E' Filkin, error on the second baseman."

It seemed like the whole City of Wheaton had been at this game. I had people kidding me, "Oh, you had a tough time playing in that championship game." Friends of mine were always giving me the rib job on all the errors and how I singlehandedly lost the game. Then, three or four weeks after the championship game I start high school and I'm scared to begin with. Everyone who had friends on the other team, that went to the other junior high schools, who I didn't even know yet by name, were making fun of me as the guy who lost the championship game.

I was so excited about being drafted for the upper league, being on the better of the two Pony Leagues that I bought a new baseball mitt—a Rawlings. There was a *Sports Illustrated* that had Bump Willis on the cover and he had a second baseman's mitt, the same as mine. He had "Bump" written on the fifth finger of his mitt. So I thought, Jeez, I ought to have my name on it—Bump can do it, I can do it. So I had Filkin placed on the fifth finger.

I worked that mitt to perfection. I was rubbing it with saddle soap and mink oil, and of course every night had it wrapped, had a ball in it, wrapped with rubber bands, underneath my mattress, and every day I'd get it out and work the folds just right. This mitt was just in immaculate condition.

To show what an impact this game had on me, I never touched the mitt again for four years. I did not play high school baseball. All my friends played baseball. Never touched the mitt, never got it out. Guys would want to play catch in the backyard; I'd find another thing to do to keep myself occupied.

STEVE **GODDARD**

Steve's dad worked for the railroad and was gone much of the time, but when he was home it was a special occasion for Steve. He was able to have a game of catch with him. It is remarkable how many of our fondest memories consist of doing something with our parents, and many times at little expense.

The movie *Field of Dreams* brought back memories to Steve. He has seen it over fifty times and never fails to cry. He is not alone.

One of the strongest memories I have of my dad is the last time we played catch. It was the fall of '64. He had bought the lot next to our house so nobody could build there, so there was plenty of room. I can still remember playing catch with him and I knew at that time he was in pain, but he played with me. I don't know what there is about playing catch with your dad. For me it was the closest I ever felt I got to him.

We didn't play that much, so when we did it was real special. He worked for the railroad. He'd be home for two days and gone for three or home for three and gone for four. It wasn't a regular schedule.

He had come in from work on Friday morning, November 20, 1964. I saw him asleep in bed that morning and he was dead by that afternoon. He had a heart attack and [died] instantly.

I felt real close to him and I felt so proud. I remember feeling that. I remember feeling so proud and how lucky I was I had a dad. I was on top of the world.

You saw the movie Field of Dreams. *At the end Kevin Costner's character asks his father, in a convoluted set of circumstances, to have a game of catch. Did this hit home?*

Oh, absolutely. I've seen the movie fifty or sixty times at least. I know it's coming and I still cry. It's that strong a movie. I'd been warned and heard that there were guys openly crying in the theatre and I couldn't believe it. When they rolled the credits in that movie I was weeping.

Some have no idea what I'm talking about and I guess those are the guys that connected with their father in a different way. I can relate to somebody more that can cry about *Field of Dreams* and understand what I'm talking about without me having to explain it. In fact, I don't think you can explain it to anybody.

Do you think there is a void in a young person's life if they have not played catch with their dad?

More important than I would have admitted six months ago, or would have even been aware of six months ago. It's really a way to connect with your father. Growing up in Oklahoma, men were real stoic and didn't say they loved you a lot—if ever. Didn't show a lot of emotions. Only saw my dad cry twice in my life that I remember: When my grandfather died and when Kennedy died. So, to play catch: Number one, you've got his time and number two, you've got his attention. That was quite a lot for me. The best I ever felt was playing catch that last time.

DAN **PETERSON**

Dan attended his first baseball game in 1945 at the age of nine and has followed the game closely ever since. He believes major league baseball is a joke, from the owners to the players to the new ballparks. He longs for the old eight team leagues, before expansion and dilution of talent.

Dan coached basketball for nearly thirty years and was considered one of Europe's foremost coaches, being named European Coach of the Year in 1987.

My complaint: Baseball as it's played today doesn't remotely compare to the game I saw played forty to fifty years ago.

Is this another gripe by another old-timer? Is this another call for the "good old days"? Believe it!

First, baseball is a team game. I once asked Enos Slaughter what he remembered most about his days with those great Cardinal teams and he said: "The teamwork, like on a fly ball to me in right. Our center fielder, Terry Moore, always ran over to tell me how much room I had and where to throw. Of course, I did the same for him." You don't see that today.

Second, baseball is a game of refined technique as opposed to natural talent. Today's players are pitiful in the skills and fundamentals of baseball. In the "old days" you worked on technique until it was perfected. It was that way or the highway. An example: While managing Brooklyn in the 1940s, Leo Durocher called up a third baseman from the minors. He wanted to see what the kid had, so he picked up a fungo and said to the youngster, "Take a hundred ground balls" and began hitting grounders to the boy.

174

Some time later the kid said, "That's a hundred!" He was counting! He knew the boy wouldn't "pay the price" and got rid of him!

As I see it, the downward slide of major league baseball began
in 1944 with the death of baseball's first commissioner, Judge
Kennesaw Mountain Landis. He'd been appointed in 1920 just
after the 1919 Black Sox scandal in which eight Chicago White
Sox players conspired to fix the 1919 World Series, purposely losing to the Cincinnati Reds.

Baseball's commissioner was all-powerful during Landis's
regime. When he handed down a lifetime ban, as he did with the
eight Black Sox, it stuck forever. He answered to no one, not to
the players, not to the owners. His only job was to safeguard the
integrity of the game, and he did just that. MLB would prosper
after an economic depression, a World War and his death thanks
to his work.

Once he was gone, though, the owners saw their chance to
take control. When Landis's successor, Kentucky Governor A. B.
"Happy" Chandler, didn't align with the owners they ousted him.
Actually it was nine votes for Chandler staying and seven against.
But he needed twelve votes of the then sixteen teams. He'd later
say, "It was the only time in my political career I had the most
votes but still lost the election." This was the early 1950s. The
power of MLB had shifted. The owners were in control.

To my way of thinking, MLB hasn't had a true commissioner
since then, but rather a series of figureheads rubber-stamping the
wishes of the owners. As sportswriter Red Smith put it when pow-
erful Walter O'Malley owned the Los Angeles Dodgers and Bowie
Kuhn was commissioner: "When Walter orders a cup of coffee,
Bowie asks if he'd like one lump of sugar or two." In any event,
with the commissioner out of the way the owners began to move.
What followed is what I call "the buying and selling of baseball."
The price of this would be the quality of the game.

Franchise moves began in 1953 when the Boston Braves
became the Milwaukee Braves. That triggered subsequent franchise shifts in rapid order. In 1954 the St. Louis Browns became
the Baltimore Orioles. In 1955 the Philadelphia A's became the

Kansas City A's. Attendance boomed and the teams improved. But little more than a decade later, the Braves were in Atlanta and the A's were in Oakland. The price for this was loyalty, fan loyalty. Wait. That sounds like it was the fans who weren't loyal. No. It was the fans who felt betrayed. None more so than those in New York in 1958, when the Brooklyn Dodgers moved to Los Angeles and the New York Giants moved to San Francisco.

In his 1993 Hall of Fame induction speech, Reggie Jackson said, "The game of Williams and Mantle and DiMaggio and Clemente" should not be overcome "by the economics." Too late, Reggie. It was too late in 1958 when John J. McGraw's Giants and Leo Durocher's Dodgers pulled up stakes and headed west.

Just days before Reggie's speech the Baltimore Orioles were auctioned off (not sold; auctioned) for $173,000,000. This put baseball's anti-trust exemption in jeopardy. For years, baseball has dodged that bullet by calling itself a game and not a business. After the Orioles' transaction, Sen. Bob Graham [D-Fla.] said, "When the Baltimore Orioles are sold for $173 million, how can baseball's owners continue to call their business a game?" Welcome aboard, Senator, albeit a bit late.

Baseball is a business and has been since the owners took power in the early fifties About that time the players, who saw things as they were, made their move to counteract the total control management had over them: They formed a union.

Before this move the players were at the mercy of management. An example, documented by David Halberstam in his book *The Summer of '49,* was how in the late forties and early fifties, Del Webb and Dan Topping, owners of the almighty New York Yankees told G. M. George Weiss he had $1 million to spend on salaries but that he could have 10% of whatever he saved against that sum. Weiss knew: Hold salaries to $600,000 and that saves $400,000; 10% of that is $40,000. A fortune for the times.

The battle lines were drawn: Owners vs. Players. The power struggle that is still going on was for baseball's dollar. To aid them in their battle the players engaged lawyer Marvin Miller. He brought the owners—and their various commissioners—to their knees. He destroyed the "Reserve Clause" that binded players to their teams even when their contracts expired. He brought about free agency with the 1975 Andy Messersmith ruling. But, as happens so often, when the pendulum swung back it didn't stop at plumb bottom. The players now had freedom of movement. The price: Loyalty to their teams. Even worse, teams could no longer *build*. No more five-year plans. No more long-range organization. Building one brick at a time was a thing of the past. Result: No more dynasties; no more long-term excellence.

Agents came on the scene in the mid-sixties. They negotiated richer contracts for their clients at the cost of team unity. No longer were players part of a twenty-five man family. Each was now a one-man corporation, answering not to who paid his salary —his team—but to who counseled him—his agent. As they say in the major league: "Twenty-five guys, twenty-five taxis."

One of the agents' biggest jobs today seems to be "damage control," when their clients run into legal trouble or have image problems. Newspapers keep score of this with a "Jurisprudence" section. MLB players keep that column busy, while the agent invariably counsels his client to repeat the words that have become so familiar: "I made a mistake, but I have to put that behind me and go forward."

Trouble is, these aren't "mistakes." A mistake is when someone doesn't know what choice to make and guesses wrong. The cases in "Jurisprudence" involve situations in which the player knows what is right and wrong. His "mistake" is getting caught.

Performance bonuses is an idea I cannot stomach. Maybe the agents didn't dream it up, but it serves their purpose. The result: The hell with the team; just put the numbers up there! With that, baseball ceases to be a team game, the game we knew in the forties and fifties. Man on second and no outs? Give myself up with a grounder to second to move my teammate to third, so he can score on a sacrifice fly, fielders choice, passed ball, wild pitch or error? Hell, no! Why hurt my batting average? Why not go for the RBI?

They even base Hall of Fame selections on "numbers." Get ready everyone: David Winfield will be in the Hall of Fame with Joe DiMaggio because he has the "numbers": 3,000 hits and 465 homers. Longevity has replaced excellence. Didn't George Steinbrenner label Winfield "Mr. May?" He was right.

I'm a Cub fan, so this hurts: Ryne Sandberg was a fine player, but no Hall of Famer. The great GM Frank Lane once said he traded Red Schoendienst for Alvin Dark because "You can win *with* Red, but not *because* of him; you win *because* of Alvin." Same with Sandberg: Wonderful player, but he's a "piece," as they say in the NBA. When Don Zimmer was fired as manager of the Cubs, he rapped Ryno, saying, "He'll steal bases, but not when you need one." Stats? Sandberg is a career .150 hitter with men in scoring position in the seventh, eighth and ninth inning. This is a Hall of Famer?

Put that up against Yogi Berra. As Chicago White Sox radio announcer Bob Elson once said of him: "Yogi may only hit .275, but in the last three innings, he hits .600!" *That* is a Hall of Famer.

Thank God they didn't measure Eddie Stanky with "performance stats." Here's Stanky's only "performance" that counts: He took three different teams to World Series [Brooklyn, Boston, New York].

The shame is that this and future generations will think MLB is a farce. They won't know that the game was once a thing of beauty: The ultimate in technical excellence and team play.

Even the stadiums and playing fields have hurt the game. Domed stadiums? You mean the "noise domes?" A travesty! Baseball is not an indoor game, period.

"Cookie-cutter" stadiums, all alike. One player said, "Sometimes I can't tell if I'm in St. Louis, Cincinnati, Pittsburgh or Philadelphia. They are all identical."

Multi-purpose stadiums? Slide the grandstand one way for football, the other way for baseball? Right. That gives us home runs off a plastic sheet instead of into a section of fans. I'll take Wrigley Field, thank you.

Artificial turf. With it no outfielder can charge a single that lands in front of him. If he does, the ball bounces over his head—hey, the "turf" is set on concrete, not dirt. So, he hangs back, waits on the ball, while baserunners take extra bases that were not there when "real" baseball was played on grass.

While I'm on stadiums, I can't put up with today's P.A. announcemers. The last good one is Bob Sheppard of the Yankees. We've traded dignity and class for FM deejays. How I miss Pat Peiper of the Cubs!

Aluminum bats haven't come to MLB, but they've worked their way up from Little League to the NCAA. Another atrocity on the beauty of the game; we've traded "crack," for "clang." Go with laminated wood bats, but stay with wood.

Official scorers today are another problem for me. Rod Beaton of *USA Today* said it best: "Many of baseball's official scorers are chicken. You see it in almost any game. If there is any doubt about a call, hit or error, they go with the hit. Score it a hit and the batter is happy, the fielder is happy."

It all comes back to performance bonuses and stats—numbers. I coached pro basketball in Italy for fourteen years. Teams gave stats bonuses for points and rebounds. Result? Those players played no defense. What? And foul out? You can't total up points and boards sitting on the bench. So those players ran up big numbers, but their teams went nowhere. Teamwork? The guy with the bonus clause shot it every time he touched it. Pass? Forget it! Our teams gave bonuses on final team placement. It was our smartest move by far. I apply my lesson to MLB. Simple as that.

The minor leagues of today are a joke compared to those of forty years ago. Today there are three classes: AAA, AA and A. There used to be *six* classes; you worked your way up, a year at a time, for six years: D, C, B, A, AA, AAA.

Back then we kids kept maps of the USA on our walls with colored pins for each affiliate of each team: a blue pin for AAA, a red one for AA, white for A, green for B, yellow for C, purple for D. We knew the Dodgers [Brooklyn] had twenty-three farm teams, the Cardinals twenty-two and so forth.

We knew kids learned the game in the minors because they were taught skills and drilled on them. We knew the Dodgers'

Branch Rickey told his minor league managers: "If you finish last, your job is safe; but if we call up a pitcher from your team and he doesn't back up third base, you'll be fired before that relay comes in!"

Today, they learn in the majors. Well, they *should* learn, but why take extra work when you are making big money and your agent is telling you how great you are? The result is today's game. To call it MAJOR LEAGUE BASEBALL galls me. The better teams of today would have placed in the second division forty years ago —in either league.

Today's MLB is vastly inferior to that played during World War II. Today's first division teams would have been second division teams in the fifties. Today's second division teams would have been AAA or AA in the fifties. And today's players, with exceptions, could not carry the bat, glove or jock of their fifties contemporaries.

What baseball needs to do is go back to sixteen teams—TOTAL! Rather than expansion, have contraction. Eight teams in the National League, eight in the American League. Let them draft from the twelve teams that are eliminated. Now we just might have something: Pitching staffs with more than two pitchers, line-ups with more than three hitters; defenses with more than four fielders. Beautiful: Three hundred and fifty guys that have no business in the majors would have to go back to the expanded minors to learn the fundamentals and team aspects of baseball.

You'll hear dissenting opinions on this. Bill Deane, formerly of the Baseball Hall of Fame, says we have enough talent, that the USA had half as many people in 1901 [when MLB went to sixteen teams] as today. Plus, he adds, MLB now draws from two previously untapped pools of talent: Black players and Latin players who came after 1946.

Wonderful. But what about sports that were next to nothing in 1946 but which siphon off gold mines of talent today: NFL football, NBA basketball, NHL hockey, even ATP tennis and PGA golf? No, sixteen is the right number—there may be enough players to flesh out sixteen MLB teams equal to those of the not-so-distant past.

In the rest of the world, in all sports, sixteen is the magic number. Ah, but there is a trick to this: "Promotion" and "Retro-
cession." Here's how it works: Cincinnati finishes last in an eight-
team National League. They then drop to AAA next year! Who
won in the AAA American Association? Louisville? Then they come
up from the minors to replace Cincy the next year. I've seen this
in operation in Europe: In soccer and in our sixteen-team Italian
Basketball League.

This system holds the league to sixteen teams, weeds out the
lesser players and lesser teams and creates a drama unknown to
U.S. sports fans. Under this setup a game between two tail-enders
in the closing days of a season is played with World Series
intensity.

MLB will go to thirty-two teams before she goes to sixteen. The
product will be polluted and milked even further. They'll call it
MLB. What a joke. Too bad the next generations won't see MLB
when it was truly that: MAJOR LEAGUE BASEBALL.

I'm glad I did.

GAR **MILLER**

is mother did not throw out his baseball cards when he was
young, therefore, he was able to build from that point to
where he now has collected over four million cards.

Remember when you could never get a Ted Williams, but were
up to your ass in Jim Delsings and Pete Castigliones?

I will trade you Bob Chakales, Jim Dyck and Thurman Tucker for
Lou Berberet, Dick Hyde and Les Moss—even up.

Tobacco companies started putting baseball cards in tobacco
as an incentive to sell cigarettes [in the 1880s]. From 1910 on they
were issued in caramels. They were issued in strips in stores. It
wasn't until 1933 that the Gouday Gum Company of Boston first
linked gum and cards together.

A penny a pack through the thirties. Gouday was the leader
in cards in the thirties. Also, National Chicle Company issued
cards, and some other companies. Play Ball Company, a
Philadelphia based company, evolved into Bowman, and issued
cards in 1939, '40 and '41.

Bowman put out their first set in 1948 and they issued cards
through 1955. It became increasingly popular for collectors, but in
terms of the hobby taking off, I don't think that happened until the
late seventies. Topps gave it new life. Of course, they had a monopoly on cards, virtually, through 1980. Topps bought Bowman out.

I collected as a kid. Started in 1948; I was ten years old. I started
accumulating cards through the early fifties, and then in 1953 my
father died and I found out that he had a collection of old tobacco
cards from 1910. He had probably a couple hundred of them. Ty

Cobb and other Hall of Famers. I found out there were other collectors around the country. Not many. I started trading, selling some, buying cards as a high school kid. I started buying my friends' cards when they were tired of collecting. There was a *Who's Who in Collecting* published in the 1950s. I was listed in the 1958 directory. There were probably only 60 or 75 collectors back then.

I stayed with it through college. I was buying cards from people who I played baseball with in college and my collection grew. Then in the late sixties I started collecting coins and let my baseball hobby go. But in the late sixties I jumped back in and really started collecting with a passion.

I started traveling the country in conjunction with my job at Atlantic Richfield Company. I traveled a lot and I would take out ads and set up at Holiday Inns and buy cards and collections. That's how I started accumulating a lot of cards.

How many cards do you have?

Oh, probably four million. There are dealers that have probably fifty million. They buy them in case lots from the manufacturers each year. I don't do a whole lot of that. I've never been a proponent of the newer cards because the manufacturers just seem to make more and more of them and they're just too many of them around. The bulk of my cards are fifties and sixties and before. I have most of the really rare cards. I have the 1933 Gouday card of [Napoleon] Lajoie. I think that's supposed to be the second rarest card.

Mint condition is overstated, but that's one man's opinion. In the last few years, as investors got into the card hobby, for better or for worse, probably for worse, they drove up the value of cards. They demanded impeccable condition cards. They got a lot of people thinking about grading and getting out magnifying glasses. Now a lot of the investors have left the hobby because they got caught holding the bag, in many cases with newer stuff that they couldn't get rid of.

Why is the Mickey Mantle card so valuable?

I guess it's 'cause Mantle's, Mantle. People can identify with him. Just an incredible baseball player. It doesn't mean that his cards are any harder to find than others. In fact, his rarest 1952 card was actually a double print in that high series. So it's not rare. I sold them years ago for as little as $10 apiece. If you look in the price guides, at one point they were listed in near mint condition for as much as $30,000 to $50,000.

Is there a market for second line ballplayers?

Sure. You have team collectors. I have a lot of people that I correspond with that are interested in putting sets together. One card of each player that was ever on a set of cards, say from the Washington Senators or the Yankees or Cleveland or whatever. A lot of people do that. A lot of people have favorite players. I heard not too long ago from Bobby Richardson's son who was trying to get some cards of him. One time I had a person that was interested in the strangest player names he could find. Eli Grba, people like that.

One constant is that the collector is still collecting. It's an opportunity for them to get cards reasonably. Prices have been driven up unrealistically high because of investors coming in looking for super grade cards. Collectors can still get quality cards. Good cards for collections that aren't necessarily in mint condition, but still collectible, and in very good condition at reasonable prices, back thirty-forty years. If you wanted to get a 1951 card of Carl Scheib of the Athletics you can probably do it for a couple of dollars. It got so that they were pushing prices of current star players [like] Frank Thomas up far more than you would pay for a forty-year-old card. It never made sense to me.

I get a kick out of some of the mistakes that the companies have made in writing the biographies on the back. My favorite was a 1964 card of Dave Bennett of the Phillies. The card said on the back, "The 16-year-old fireballing right hander is only 18." There have been a lot of goofs—the Billy Ripken bat with the obscenity painted on the end that they had to re-issue.

I was one of the people who at an early stage was maybe one of the pioneers, but there are a lot of people in that category. I did write the first how-to-collect book in 1973 with a price guide, before there were any price guides. Jim Beckett started publishing a price guide, which has become a multi-million dollar business for him.

It's a hobby I have enjoyed because I've been so close to baseball as a player, as a sportswriter. As a fanatic, really, about the game. I had a story published in the *1975 Phillies Year Book* called "Confessions of a Super Fan." In it I talked about going to incredible lengths to follow my team. I subscribed to the Eugene, Oregon *Register Guardian* for a year to follow the minor league team. I traveled to Redding to watch the Redding Phillies.

I still am a big baseball fan and the cards have been a part of it. I had a good job with Atlantic Richfield and that was enough for me.

OUTSIDE THE LINES

JONATHAN **WINTERS**

D on't miss the mortgage payment, don't call Gloria
Steinem a "chick," and don't mess with "Bad Boy"
Lenderhoffer.

*We're talking today with "Bad Boy" Lenderhoffer. His real name
is Al Lenderhoffer. Al, how did you come by the name of "Bad
Boy"? I assume that you are a bad boy.*
    Well, not only was I a bad boy, but I am, today, a bad adult.

*Well, wait a minute. You're not talking about having been in a
detention home and done one to five or something. In other words,
criminal things?*
    No, not criminal things, per se. I have certainly never, to my
knowledge, murdered anybody. I was in the war and I killed
some people out there. If you want to classify that as murder, I
got a medal for that. I killed about—oh, between fifteen and
twenty Japanese. I mean, my back was against a mountain and
they come up on me and they was all laughin' and jeerin'.
    I was in the Marines and my buddies was all, you know, blown
to bits and everything. I don't like to delve on it because it was
a time of my life I'm still trying to erase—but since you brought
it up, I had a machine gun. I was a machine gunner. That's what
I was trained to do. We was taught to kill. In a war you just don't
always have a parade, and there's not always a victory or a defeat.
There's a lot of killing in between. Otherwise, it's a bum war. So,
at any rate, I killed about—what'd I tell you?

Well, you said something about twenty.

That's about right. It was about eighteen to twenty. It's not a question of being proud of it. I did my job. I got rid of them and right shortly after that I got a medal from—I forget the general right now. I've had some problems, I'm getting on in age. But, I was laying in a hospital and one guy tried to cut my boots off. And, so, next thing I knowed the general come in and give me what was close to the Medal of Honor. He said, "I would give you that, but if you'd a had one more, you'd have got the Medal of Honor." Isn't that something, you know? Get that many—thirteen at once, or what did I say, twenty?

Let's keep it at twenty. That's plenty.

No, it isn't. 'Cause if I had twenty-one, I'd had the Medal of Honor. This way I got the Silver Star. Then I got the Navy Medal. Should of got the Purple Heart for the guy cutting the boot.

Well, let's get on with your baseball. Obviously, you didn't get a chance to play much baseball when you were in the service.

No, and it was a shame too. 'Cause I really wanted to play ball. It wasn't that I was wanting to stay home. I wanted to go overseas. I wanted to go overseas so much that they sent me overseas. I mean, if you keep saying, "I want to go overseas," sooner or later they'll get you there. Well, when I come back and got discharged I had problems with my mind at that time, you know . . . and . . .

Well, let's get back here for a moment. I mean, we're skipping around a little bit. This nickname "Bad Boy." When did that come about?

Oh, okay. That's when I was a kid. And . . .

Where are you from originally, "Bad Boy"?

Originally, from Lengler. Lengler, Kentucky and then I moved into Ohio.

When you were a kid, what happened to the label of "Bad Boy"?

Well, in Lengler we just had sandlot ball. We had chicken wire for a backstop and my aunt's pillows. Three of them and we filled them full of sand. One was Niagara Falls. Second base I always remember just had "Ohio" on it. And then the third pillow was plain. They was bases.

One day Bobby Frickser—Bobby was pitching to me—I was always one for stepping in a little close to the plate. And he said, "If you step one step closer to that plate, I'll bean you with this ball." Well, he did. In those days, we're going back fifty-sixty years, we didn't have no liners. Didn't have no protection over our ear or nothing, and I dropped. I thought my brain had been broke. As a matter of fact, I had hairline fractures throughout my entire skull. I think it was a matter of five to ten minutes I lay there and both teams unload the benches. They was interested in fighting among themselves—not over my bent head. And then he bent over me, the boy that throwed that ball. I said "Oh, you shouldn't have did that." I picked up a Louisville Slugger and I hit him as hard as I could. And he's never been right. He's just setting on a chair now on his porch in Toll Valley, Arkansas. He just sits there and looks out at the stream or whatever. I meant to kill him. So from then on they called me "Bad Boy."

I was "Bad Boy" in the Marines and I'm a "Bad Boy" today, only I'm just a "Bad Ole Man," you know. I just won't take crap from anybody. I carry a bat with me. I'm not one for carryin' a gun. I carry a bat. I've had people try to break into my car and I just use that bat, boy, and it works. You hit a guy in the back with that bat and he'll look like he's looking for shells the rest of his life, I'll tell you that.

Did you play AA or AAA?

I skipped AA. I went right to AAA. I quit high school. I was a little older than Joe Nuxhall when I come into the National League. I went into the American League. Then I went to AA and I stayed there. I was up in the majors—I was three years in the National League with the Reds, Cubs, Cards, Dodgers and Braves.

What was the problem?

I was a bad boy. "Bad boy," they'd say, "here comes 'bad boy'." I'd last maybe a year. They knew I was bad news. But I had developed a way to stand and a way to hit.

What was your lifetime batting average?

It was .112. But when I hit—I know you're going to laugh and everything—when I hit the ball, it went out.

Well, obviously, with a batting average of .112, you didn't hit many out!

No, I didn't. So what. And if you get me mad—I carry a bat with me. You didn't listen to me. You want me to hit you now?

No, I certainly don't. Please. Well now, you were with the National League, then you went on to the American League.

Yeah, I was with the Yankees for a while. I was with the Baltimore Orioles, Chicago White Sox, the Senators. I played with almost everybody. I was always a misfit. And it all goes back to that kid. If he hadn't hit me I would never have that label of "Bad Boy."

Are you married?

No. Everybody I have are just friends. I've got five to ten women friends up the street. I've got two buddies down here that suck on beer all day and listen to the *Young and Restless* and go through baseball magazines.

What a marvelous time and opportunity it has been to talk to you and . . .

Well, what do I get? Is there any money involved? Something to cross my palm other than Tupperware?

Other than Tupperware? Certainly a copy of the book that I'm finishing here. This is the end of our interview. There's a box of candy.

I'm a diabetic.

Well, take it and maybe you can go to sleep. At any rate, good luck and we'll be giving you a lifetime pass to Chevron Stations.

RICHARD **TOPP**

He is past president of the Society for American Baseball Research—also known as **SABR**. They research everything possible in the baseball universe; virtually nothing is too irrelevant for them.

Richard has been researching baseball deaths for many years.

SABR was founded in 1971. It's made up of people from all walks of life, and they're preserving the history of the national pasttime. We have roughly 6,000 members. You can find research on any facet of baseball. If you want research on women's baseball of the 1880s in Delaware, somebody's doin' it, somebody did it. Or some Class D league in 1912, somebody's researched it. We've done nicknames, uniforms. One of our members did a complete uniform book, every uniform in the twentieth century in full color. We have a ballparks committee, a biographical committee, bibliography committee. You name it—we have it. Everything from baseball fiction, to my forte which is death. We have a convention once a year—have regional meetings.

There's a guy named John Dodge who played in the majors in 1912 and 1913. He was a major leaguer, but he went down. He was hit in the throat with a baseball playing with Mobile—was killed. There was another major leaguer who became an umpire. He also was hit in the throat with a baseball. At least four minor leaguers have been killed by pitched balls, the last one in 1951—Ottis Johnson. There's another guy who played opening day with the Philadelphia A's. He crashed into a wall and developed a burst appendix a few days later and died. He was an outfielder.

Violent deaths! A guy named John Ryan—1902. He plays in the 1880s but in 1902 he's a policeman in Philadelphia. He is literally kicked to death while making an arrest.

Suicide—Don Bessent in Jacksonville, Florida. This is a couple of years ago. He is dying of cirrhosis of the liver. He gets in his car, pulls into a parking lot at a local Wendy's and proceeds to drink a bottle of rubbing alcohol. What a way to go, huh?

Another one is Fritz Bratschi—he played with the White Sox and Boston in the twenties. He's dying of cancer in the 1960s. He goes into his garage in Massillon, Ohio, pops open the hood of his Chevy, takes out the battery and drinks battery acid.

Willard Hershberger [Cincinnati] was subbing for the injured Ernie Lombardi during the 1940 pennant race and he was so tense in his hotel room in Boston he committed suicide. Slashed his wrists in the bathtub.

The most gruesome suicide [was] Marty Bergen. Marty is catching for Boston in 1899 in the last game of the season, he's blocking home plate and breaks his hip. In January 1900 he does a Lizzie Borden number on his wife and two daughters and then cuts his throat.

Not a death, but close to it, was Eddie Waitkus being shot by Ruth Ann Steinhagen.

Yeah, that was 1949. She was obsessed with him. She was a 19-year-old bobbie soxer. Waitkus just got traded from the Cubs to the Phillies. She gets a room at the Edgewater Beach Hotel [in Chicago] and coerces Waitkus to come to her room and shoots him in the chest with a .22 caliber rifle.

There was another one. Billy Herman also got nailed—by a woman named Popovich. I believe it was at the Hotel Carlos, which is about a block north of Wrigley Field. That's also the same hotel where pitcher Hal Carlson [of the Cubs] died between games of a doubleheader. He had a stomach disorder.

Eddie Gaedel was the midget Bill Veeck had pinch-hit in 1951. He died a violent death.

Bob Cain [Detroit pitcher], when he came back to the dugout, Dizzy Trout says, "You should have hit the little son of a bitch." He was coming out of a bar and he was bludgeoned—had the crap beat out of him by two street thugs. He went home, had a heart attack and died. Died very quietly. Practically unnoticed in the paper.

Right after he did his little routine with the St. Louis Browns, he was arrested in Cincinnati, Ohio—he was a circus midget or a carnival midget—for punching out a cab driver. My kind of guy.

Len Koenecke. He dies in 1935. He was sent down by the Brooklyn Dodgers and he had to make a game in Toronto. The paper said he was drunk and disorderly in a private plane and tried to take over the plane. The real story is that he made a homosexual advance to the pilot and the co-pilot hit him in the head with a fire extinguisher. They landed on the infield of a race-track outside Toronto. The story was in the Royal Canadian Mounted Police report.

We've got guys burning to death, falling down a flight of stairs. Oh, we've got one guy—a guy named Lyons. He was asphyxiated by his dentist. His mouth was full of cotton and the dentist was giving him gas and the dentist misjudged it and suffocated the guy.

We've got a couple of guys asphyxiated by gas in their hotel rooms. We've got Charlie Snyder who was thrown out of his hotel owing money for drinks and hit his head on the sidewalk. He died on the sidewalk. Fractured his skull while being evicted from a hotel in 1901.

Who was the youngest major leaguer to die?

That was Jay Dahl. He played in '63 with the Houston Colts. He's 19 years old when he dies. Auto accident. He played in only one game.

Kenny Hubbs. He went out on an airplane, he had a pilot's license for two weeks, and took off in a snow storm. Smashed his Cessna into a frozen lake near Provo, Utah. He was Rookie of the Year in '62.

Chris Hartje. He caught eight games for the Dodgers in '39. In 1946 he's playing with Spokane in the Pacific Coast League and [he and] eight players die in a bus accident.

MARVIN **MILLER**

As the founding Executive Director of the Major League Baseball Players Association, he changed the economics of baseball. He was instrumental in winning the Andy Messersmith arbitration case that challenged baseball's time honored reserve clause. The reserve clause literally bound a player to his team in perpetuity. He won the case, resulting in free agency, and the financial benefit the players presently enjoy. A lot of guys owe him big time.

In the forties, an organization was formed called the Major League Baseball Players Association, but it was formed by the owners, not the players. The idea was to head off legitimate unionism and not to create a trade union. You may remember what had happened in the forties. Two wealthy Mexican brothers formed a league in Mexico by urging star players to leave the United States and play in the newly created Mexican League. The owners were trying to put a stop to that. They did not know how successful that might be.

At that time Robert Murphy who had been a field examiner for the National Labor Relations Board, a Harvard-trained lawyer, decided apparently on his own to try to organize the players. In the spring of 1947 he traveled to various spring training camps trying to organize the players, developing a program of demanding a minimum salary for the first time in the major leagues, a spring training allowance to pay expenses because players didn't draw salaries during spring training and a demand for a pension plan and for representation.

So the owners, trying to avoid losing players to the Mexican League, and also trying to avoid organization of the players to what Murphy called the American Baseball Guild, decided that they would form a company union, and that's exactly what they did. They formed an organization and decreed that there would be a player representative from each club. They then, in the fashion of those days, told the players who the player representative should be from each club, and then for I don't know how many years met with those player representatives once a year, usually about the time of the winter meeting in New York. This was a caricature of how you try to prevent unionism by forming a company union.

In the early sixties, players, not a great number, but some veteran players who were sick and tired of the runaround they had been getting for years, decided to form their own organization. They created a budget for a legitimate players' association; they created a search committee to find an appropriate person to be executive director; they began talking to recognized experts in the labor management field and so on. And through a whole series of events, which now seem quite improbable even to me, the union got started in mid-1966.

As the founding director of the Major League Baseball Players' Association, you were involved with the Curt Flood case.

The Flood case did not erupt until three-and-a-half years later. The Flood case was something that could not have happened and could not have been developed if the preceding events had not occurred, that is, the forming of the Players' Association as a legitimate union. Because Flood would have had nobody to help with the financing, nobody to see to it that appropriate anti-trust lawyers were retained, and so on. It would not have happened if the preceding event of having formed the Players' Association in 1966 had not taken place.

Curt Flood was trying to strike the reserve clause which, in effect, meant that ballplayers were bound to ball clubs forever. He lost

*and, in fact, it went to the Supreme Court and he again lost on
a vote of five to three.*

That's true. I have always described it as a loss, which it obviously was in one sense. But in recent years I've reconsidered my
judgment of it. I don't think a case that educated so many people as to what the reserve rules were, and how horrible, and
which eventually led to an arbitration decision striking it down,
I don't think any such case can be declared a loser. At worst you
can describe it as a temporary setback.

*The decision was the result of the Andy Messersmith arbitration
of 1975 and the arbitrator was Peter Seitz.*

Seitz was the permanent arbitrator agreed on by both sides, not
just for that case, but for a fairly extensive period. I think he
grasped more than most arbitrators would have. He understood
that this was a hallmark case, not just another grievance, and that
this could, depending upon his decision, change the entire course
of the industry. Not many grievances that go to arbitration have
that kind of impact. He understood that almost immediately and
as a result decided that even though it's not usually the role of
an arbitrator in modern times to step out of character and attempt
to encourage the parties to withdraw the case from arbitration and
settle it themselves, he took that rather extraordinary step and in
the middle of the case attempted to get the parties to agree to
settle it themselves and let him out of it. A very perceptive and
courageous act for which he never got enough credit because the
people covering it did not understand the nuances of labor-man-
agement arbitration.

*Messersmith wanted a "no-trade" clause in his contract. This is
what precipitated it.*

Exactly. Andy Messersmith was, and as far as I know is, a very
honorable man. In his relationship with O'Malley, the dispute
between them started out as a salary dispute and went a little further in the sense that Messersmith had already been traded once
in his career to the Dodgers. He didn't want to leave California.

It's ironic, he simply wanted to ensure that he would stay with the Dodgers.

He called me when the grievance was about to be filed to alert me to what his feelings were. His feeling was that if the Dodgers met his terms, then he would feel honor-bound to withdraw the grievance. They had already agreed to his salary figure. All that stood in the way was the demand for a no-trade clause, which they had so far not given, but he wanted to make sure I understood that if they gave in on that there would be no case. I said, "Okay." A man tells me that's his commitment and that's the way he's going to act, that's fine. What I did after that was call Dave McNally.

That's how McNally got into this case. I assured Messersmith that I understood and that he was free to withdraw the case and that I understood why he would do it if they met his terms. I simply called the only other player that was in that same or relatively same position. That is, who had not signed a contract for the forthcoming year, or for the prior year. I explained to McNally what had happened and simply asked if he would be willing in case Messersmith's terms were met and [he] withdrew, that this adjudication would continue. And McNally said, "Fine." So the grievance was amended to include McNally.

It is ironic. Here is a man that simply did not want to be traded, and from there it proceeds to change the face of baseball. The salaries players receive today are a result of your work. You point out in your book A Whole Different Ball Game *that people resent these salaries because they have played baseball themselves— "I played the game; why should they be paid so much?"*

There is both identification and non-identification with this kind of money. You're quite right. I want to mention one thing, though. That while you're right, there is some resentment, and initially there was even more resentment among the old-time top stars about today's salaries—it isn't true of many of the "class" players. I particularly remember DiMaggio's comment when asked, "Don't you think these players are all overpaid compared to what you got?" DiMaggio said, "No, we were underpaid."

It was frustrating dealing with Bowie Kuhn. I never considered him a bad man. I considered him as somebody who was less than intelligent. I think he was somebody who really, like many other commissioners—if not every other commissioner— just misperceived that his role was waterboy to the owners and never understanding the relationship of forces. The owners—certainly not all of them are dunderheads—I thought O'Malley was one of the really bright businessmen I had ever met. And others, too. Charlie Finley, while he was a pain in the ass to a lot of people, I think he was never given enough credit for being one of the most perceptive talent scouts among owners of all time. People don't understand that Charlie Finley in an age where scouting was handed off to so-called experts was his own talent scout. He was his own general manager and his own everything. He extended himself too far, but put together three World Series Champions in a row.

The players owe you a tremendous debt. Do they appreciate what you did?

Oh, no. No. But on the other hand, I'm not sure that that's different than in other walks of life. I'll give you a couple of anecdotes.

Not too long ago, there was a survey done at a community college here where a majority of the people are black. One of the questions asked in the survey was, "Who was Martin Luther King, Jr.," and I forgot the figure, but a tiny percentage could identify him.

I remember in my days in Pittsburgh, Phillip Murray had been a vice president of the Mine Workers Union and then the president of the Steelworkers Organizing Committee and then the president of the Steelworkers Union and then replaced [John L.] Lewis as president of the CIO and was a major figure in the labor movement. He died in 1952 and a couple of years later a new junior high school was built in Pittsburgh and named "The Phillip Murray

Junior High." A few years after that a newspaper guy with maybe a sense of humor surveyed the students and faculty as to who was Phillip Murray. A tiny percentage could identify him. So, it's not just me, it's not just baseball players, it's the human condition.

DICK **MOSS**

He is considered one of the best agents in baseball. Dick comes to the job well qualified, once being Associate General Counsel for the Steelworkers' Union. He also worked with Marvin Miller as General Counsel for the Major League Baseball Players Association.

I'm a labor lawyer by background. I was Associate General Counsel for the Steelworkers' Union in Pittsburgh when Marvin [Miller] was elected head of the Players Association to try to make it something other than a company union. He asked me to come along as General Counsel in 1967. I served as General Counsel for the Players Association until the middle of 1977. During that time the office was a little different than it is now. There were just the two of us and two secretaries, but we got a fair amount accomplished.

I left in 1977. I guess I was sort of having a midlife crisis and there were a number of things I wanted to do, one of which was to represent a few players to show all those goddamned agents out there how it should be done. I found that representing players was a lot of fun.

My first client, who called me the day after I left the Players Association, was Dan Spillner, then a pitcher for the San Diego Padres, and he has always been very special to me for that reason. The next day I got a call from Larry Hisle who was with Minnesota but was about to become a free agent, and turned out that he was the biggest free agent that year. So we had some fun with that.

I'll represent anybody I feel like I can be [of] some help to. I have been lucky over the years in that I've had almost without exception nice clients, nice people to represent. I guess if there's a qualification, that's it.

Will the players take part in the negotiation with you?

Oh, sure, if he's comfortable doing so. I think it is a great advantage to have him there. There are some players that would not want to be part of that, but that's rare, and the usual case is that I involve players in the negotiations directly.

Statistics are important if you're trying a salary arbitration case. It becomes very important then, but not nearly as important in private negotiations. You're dealing at that point with knowledge of the player and his assets, not only statistically, but otherwise, and the needs of the club.

One of the reason baseball's such a wonderful game is that there are so many statistics out there readily available to everybody. You really don't have to do a lot of work keeping up on them. But you have to be aware of the statistics and how each player's performance compares to other players.

The usefulness of a player in negotiations is to talk about his playing abilities, to demonstrate his competitiveness, his eagerness to play for that team, the assets he has. The player doesn't usually do what I do, which is to try to make a bargain. The secret of negotiating, whether it's for a player or anything else, is to find out what the other guy needs and try to accommodate him and get what you want in the process. I don't mind being the bad guy if that helps accomplish the goal.

The biggest deal at the time was when Nolan Ryan became a free agent with California and wanted to go home to Texas, and John McMullen had just bought the Houston club. I negotiated with McMullen and we made a deal that made Nolan the first million-dollar-a-year player in professional team sports. But I'll never forget the night that we finished it. We were having dinner together and I took out a pad and I was writing down what our agreement was going to be so we could sign off on it that evening. We went over the salaries, and the bonuses and so on and so forth, and we got to the end and I said, "John, there's one other item that I'm a little reluctant to ask you about. I do only because Nolan had this with the Angels, but I'd like to put in here that the club will pay for a single room on the road during the season." John said, "Absolutely not, I'm going to put my foot down here, I will not do that. But, I'll tell you what I'll do instead, I will see to it that during the length of this contract, whenever my financial advisers offer me a deal to get into, I'll make it available to Nolan too." Then he said, "I think it's only right to do that because after all he's going to be making almost as much money as I'm making." I had just made this great big deal, and set some precedent. He put it all in context: almost as much money as he makes. That was one of the more satisfying ones.

The Valenzuela arbitration in 1982 was the first million-dollar arbitration case [and] was significant. Gary Carter's seven-year contract making him the first player to have a contract averaging over two million dollars a year.

Major league salaries and benefits make up a little over 40% [of the payroll]. But you also have to bear in mind this is not a usual industry. These players are more than employees. They are the product that's being sold. So, if anything, it should be a greater percentage.

This is a very big and profitable industry. Every source of revenue has just mushroomed, including ticket prices and concessions. But one of the most remarkable things is how big merchandizing has become. These people make a fortune in licensing their logos and other baseball-related matters.

I always get a kick out of the Dodgers who brag year after year that they've got the lowest ticket prices in baseball. That's true, but they also have the highest hot dog prices in baseball.

There is a natural tendency in a sport or industry like this to look to franchise players to lead the way and to fill in the rest of the team with competent people. If there's a choice between a younger player, with a lower salary, and an older player, whose salary has built up over the years, and their talents are equal, there will always be a tendency to go with the younger player. I don't see anything sinister in that. I think that's natural.

The networks are becoming less and less significant in television and that's why they can't pay as much as they used to pay—or think they can't. On the other hand, cable television rates keep going up and up and up. As I mentioned before, national television is only one of many, many, many, many sources of revenue and every other single source of revenue is mushrooming. So these people who are trying to put down their own industry and say, "We're in trouble," have no factual basis for doing that. In addition, the stupidity of doing that when you're trying to sell a product. Contrast that with basketball and the way basketball owners promote their star players. You don't see that in baseball. It's outrageous.

What are the differences in players today as opposed to twenty years ago?

There is a difference, although there are a lot of similarities, too. In the main, more similarities than differences. The players today are a little more dedicated. Dedicated in their work ethic, in being in shape. That wasn't the case in the fifties and the sixties; today, every player goes to spring training in shape. Spring training is not to get into shape. The biggest reason for that is the money. There's a lot at stake now and players are a lot more serious about the game than they were in the past.

CURT **SMITH**

B roadcasting a baseball game is an art. There are few that have done it well. But those that have are in a class by themselves: Red Barber, Mel Allen, Dizzy Dean, Russ Hodges, Jack Buck, Harry Caray and Vin Scully are, and were, as popular as the players they covered.

Curt Smith is the author of *Voices of The Game*, a comprehensive study of the men who have broadcast baseball since the Harding administration.

On August 5, 1921 Harold Arlin broadcast the first baseball game from Forbes Field, Pittsburgh over radio station KDKA. The Pirates beat the Phillies 8-5. Did people realize that this was a major breakthrough, or did they think it was a fad?

No one knew. Harold Arlin has noted that on that August day when he went to Forbes Field he didn't know what he was doing since no one had ever done play-by-play. He went with a carbon microphone, a plank of wood and a scorebook. Those were his items of equipment. He didn't know if anyone was listening. There were a minute number of sets in America at that time.

Arlin was a Westinghouse Company foreman and worked at Westinghouse by night and broadcast baseball by day. He was a pioneer and forty-five years later he came back to Forbes Field and did an inning of Pirates play-by-play with Bob Prince, the voice of the Pirates, and wondered of the enormous changes which had engulfed radio and television.

Nineteen twenty-three was radio's breakthrough year for World Series coverage. [Graham]) McNamee did the play-by-play to several stations. All throughout the 1920s, and indeed through 1933, McNamee did the play-by-play and spiraled into the nation's most prominent announcer. He did baseball, college football, boxing, political conventions. He knew that radio was reaching the masses when in 1925, within a week after the Pirates-Senators World Series, 50,000 letters swamped the NBC offices in New York.

All throughout the twenties and thirties baseball broadcasting was erratic, spotty and very regionalized. In Chicago, for instance, at one point in the 1920s, seven different stations simultaneously carried Cubs games. On the other hand, not until 1939 did any radio baseball grace New York City. Many owners, including the owners in New York, were deathly afraid that no one would pay to go to games that they could hear for free; did not realize that radio indeed could assist attendance, not retard it.

New York City was the last major league market to have radio. However, when they did begin, they began in a grand way with Red Barber at Brooklyn and Mel Allen at the Polo Grounds and Yankee Stadium.

A radio station in Des Moines, WHO, would do re-creations by a broadcaster by the name of Ron Reagan. They paid no fees for rights. It was only a matter of time before major league teams would insist upon rights fees and stations would insist upon exclusivity.

It [broadcasting] began to develop in the thirties, again on a spotty basis—market by market, very regionalized. Red Barber's first year in Cincinnati, 1934, three stations did Reds games. Barber was so good that he quickly drove out the other two competing stations. In Pittsburgh there was only one, KDKA, that did games. St. Louis, in the mid-1940s, Harry Caray and Gabby Street did broadcasts on one station, France Laux on another, Dizzy Dean on a third.

You mentioned re-creations. Until the late forties, early fifties, most major league teams did away games by re-creation. In other words, they took it right off the Western Union wire.

The Yankees were the first team to do all games live in 1946. Mel Allen came to Yankee Stadium, back from the war, and became the first broadcaster to do all games live, all 154 games. The Pirates, in 1956 I believe, were the last team to abandon re-creations. Re-creations evolved for the simplest of reasons: it was prohibitive financially to send announcers on road trips. It was much cheaper to sit the announcer in a studio in the home city and get the wire reports over the ticker and then translate that skeletal information into play-by-play.

Dizzy Dean was the most entertaining broadcaster that I've ever heard. My first book was *America's Dizzy Dean,* and his impact was enormous. He was really the first ex-athlete to make it big as an announcer. He was the first broadcaster to consciously inject humor into the game. He became bigger than the game itself. He didn't give you balls and strikes except by accident. He butchered the English language, talking about a runner who "slud" into third, or a batter who "swang" at the ball, or a pitcher who "throwed" a pitch, or saying of several runners they are returning to their "respectable" positions, or saying a hitter is standing "confidentially" at the plate. I remember when growing up in upstate New York how he would sing "The Wabash Cannonball" weekly. He was the show, the essence of the first network television series on a weekly basis in any sport—the 1955 through '65 *Game of the Week.* Extraordinarily important because this was the precursor to all of the network television that we have now in every sport. His series was gigantically successful because Dean was gigantically popular.

The *Game of the Week* was interesting because it did not come into major league cities; they were blacked out. More than half of America did not have access to major league baseball televised locally, so the *Game of the Week* went largely into the South, the West, rural areas. Dizzy Dean made baseball a religion in small-town America. There has never been another like him. He is a pivotal figure without doubt or question in the history of radio/television broadcasting.

One of the joys of baseball broadcasting is that it is like any index of entertainment: it's very subjective. We all have favorites.

What means chocolate to me may mean vanilla to you. It's subjective, it's emotional, no one is really right nor wrong.

I think to be a great broadcaster one must have the resonant voice that will inject a sense of drama. You have to have an appreciation of baseball, to love the game. Understand its poetry, its ambiance, its drama and attention to detail. You have to be able to tell stories, to intersperse anecdotes with play-by-play. When it's two to one, you can focus on balls and strikes; when it's twenty to two you damn well better be able to tell stories and to entertain. I think a sense of humor helps as well.

With that as a criteria, I would flip a coin: greatest ever—Allen, Barber or Vin Scully. I refer to Roy Hobbs in the movie *The Natural* when he says "the best there ever was." To me, Mel Allen is the best there ever was. No question about it.

Mel Allen was an institution, covering the Yankees from 1939 through 1965. But he was fired. Why?

No one will ever know. Reasons that are given are sheer conjecture, and I would not purport to surmise because I don't know. I accept Allen's explanation. Ballantine Beer was the Yankees' main sponsor. Allen had a very large salary. Ballantine at that point was going bankrupt and would indeed cease to exist in the next decade. Ballantine apparently felt the easiest way they could cut expenses was by erasing the largest salary they paid, and that was to Mel Allen. This is what Mel says and I accept that explanation. The decision hurt Mel a great deal, but it hurt the Yankees more. It took the Yankees years to recover from the public relations debacle of firing the best announcer in baseball, and frankly, the most famous announcer in sports. One of the most famous broadcasters in the world.

Variety magazine did a poll in the 1950s and of the twenty-five most recognizable voices in the world, Allen was the only broadcaster. Sad story, but it has a happy ending, that through *This Week In Baseball* and other broadcast ventures, Allen over the years staged a comeback to where once again he was an extraordinarily recognizable name.

Who do you feel were, and are, the greatest voices of the game?

This is very subjective, but it's a good question. In fact, I gave the *Miami Herald* a list:

Allen.

Dean.

Scully, whom I call the Lawrence Olivier of baseball broadcasting.

Barber.

McNamee, because he was the first nationally known baseball broadcaster.

Harry Caray, enormously important. Has owned the midwest for half a century. The Jackie Gleason of baseball broadcasting.

Bob Prince of the Pirates, except for Dean the most entertaining announcer that I have ever heard.

Harwell is one of the best. Ernie Harwell is the most honorable man I've ever met in sport. A terrific announcer and one of the many great southern voices.

It's interesting how many of the great broadcasters come from the South. Allen, Dean, Barber, Jimmy Dudley—another fine announcer. Lindsey Nelson. Lindsey Nelson has to be on anyone's list of the all-time great.

The southern voice tends to be soothing, informal, old shoe, lyrical, poetic. Well, that's baseball. The voice fits the game. Also, I think the South has been justifiably called America's great moral storytelling region. It has a tradition of anecdotes. Anecdotes fit no sport better than baseball. There's a great deal of dead space between pitches. Those that can spin yarns, keep you amused, tell a story, tend to flourish best. That's the South and that's people like Nelson, Dean, Allen and Barber.

"THERE USED TO BE A BALLPARK"

Frank Sinatra recorded this song in the summer of 1973 after his premature retirement in 1971. Joe Raposo, a songwriter from New York, wrote the piece and it was included in Sinatra's album "Ol' Blue Eyes Is Back," released in the fall of 1973.

The song contains some strong messages. Using baseball as a metaphor for life, he comments on the lack of caring, commitment, and growing older.

It is a sentimental look back to the "old days" when life was simpler. Listening, you can almost smell the wooden benches in the sun, hear the shouting and taste the beer and the hot dogs. This is one of the most moving songs I have ever heard.

> And there used to be a ballpark
> Where the field was warm and green
> And the people played their crazy game
> With a joy I'd never seen
> And the air was such a wonder
> From the hot dogs and the beer
> Yes, there used to be a ballpark right here.
>
> And there used to be rock candy
> and a great big Fourth of July
> With the fireworks exploding
> All across the summer sky
> And the people watched in wonder
> How they laughed and how they cheered
> And there used to be a ballpark right here.

Now the children try to find it
And they can't believe their eyes
'Cause the old team just isn't playing
And the new team hardly tries
And the sky has got so cloudy
When it used to be so clear
And the summer went so quickly this year.

Yes, there used to be a ballpark . . . right here.

THERE USED TO BE A BALLPARK—Words and music: Joe Raposo © 1973 Jonico Music, Inc. and Sergeant Music Co. Used by permission.

EPILOGUE

EPILOGUE

Enos Slaughter was a hero when he raced home from first on a double by Harry Walker in the eighth inning of the seventh game of the 1946 World Series, winning the Series for St. Louis. But in the context of that time, America had larger heroes: Men and women who had survived a depression, had fought in World War II and now were bringing home $60 a week to feed their family and replace the bald tires on the '38 Ford. People then were not confusing Slaughter's 270-foot sprint with Omaha Beach or Tarawa; celebrity was kept in proper perspective. Sports hyperbole, puffery, and distortion lay incubating, to be hatched later by fifties embourgeoisment and television largess.

Perspectives change with time, not only social, economic and political, but also sports, particularly baseball. For many who viewed baseball during the "Golden Era" of 1946 to 1960, the game today no longer has the same resonance. Their mental album of baseball memories includes day baseball, Slaughter, Durocher, Thomson, Mantle, seventy-five-cent bleacher seats, worn baseballs wrapped with tape tighter than Tutankhamen and two-dollar baseball gloves.

The next generation grew up with Little League and Pony League, baseball gloves weighing more than a real estate closing, players charging the pitcher like enraged Serbs when brushed back, games played mostly at night and lasting longer than Pauly Shore's career, a $100 tab for a family of four to attend a major league game and players who destroy their careers and lives by pursuing drugs and other criminal behavior.

The abolition of the Reserve Clause in 1975 liberated the players, giving them the ability to bargain with other teams, eventually evolving into "rent-a-players" with large salaries. Baseball became marketed because of television as entertainment rather than sport, and many in the game postured accordingly, any prolonged encounter with them leaving you deeply disappointed.

Some in the game are not worth much, but the game is. After the strike and cancellation of the World Series, with Ruthian timing, Mark McGwire and Sammy Sosa reversed baseball's downward spiral, adding life, energy and luster to a game that had come to produce mostly complaints. A game devouring endless hours, fans who behave as if attending Oktoberfest, players who are nouveau and witless, owners who operate on Bering time and have the conscience of a Chicago alderman.

Baseball has survived the Federal League, the Black Sox, the Depression, World War II, Expansion, the Reserve Clause and its demise, and conflicts between the players and owners worthy of the UAW and GM. Baseball builds and maintains a constituency no matter its problems because it affords us the opportunity to observe a select group, play a difficult game, executing unique skills the rest of us do not possess. This is the heart of the baseball experience.

But baseball is more: Those who played under difficult circumstances, never complaining, feeling blessed to be part of the game. The stars, journeymen, the dedicated and the flakes. Those fortunate enough to make history, the majority whom history forgot. The content, the bitter, the rich and poor, those with a crowded past, those with thin yesterdays. The over-achievers, the lazy and aggressively mediocre, those whose hopes were realized, the many whose hopes were dashed. The proud, the fading.

A nation of wannabes who do not progress past sandlot baseball, those who were not chosen to play, those told to play right field. Fans who obsess over their team, the bleacher bums, Wrigley, Fenway and Yankee Stadium, Red, Mel and Vin. Roger Kahn and the cub sports reporter. Klem, Jocko and Al. The genius of Phil Alden Robinson. Joe E. Brown, Gary Cooper, Bill Bendix,

Jimmy Stewart, Ray Milland, Paul Douglas, Dan Dailey, Ronald Reagan, Robert Redford and Kevin Costner. Your mother who kept your baseball cards, your dad who after a hard day at work never said "no" to a game of catch. The stats, box scores, gossip and hype. Rawlings, Wilson, Spaulding, Louisville and Adirondack. McGwire, Sosa, spectacular plays, no-hitters. Uniforms and hats as ugly as Gary, Indiana. Managers who make a chump out of Darwin, owners who convince us that self-interest is not a recessive gene. Players who are famous, but not important. The hundreds of thousands who have played in the minors only to discover they had peaked at eighteen.

A game whose hold on America can be traced back to millions playing baseball as children, teaching the game to their children, culminating in a game of catch with their grandchildren. I cannot think of a better journey.